IT Problem
Management

ISBN 0-13-030770-X

9 780130 307705

90000

HARRIS KERN'S ENTERPRISE COMPUTING INSTITUTE

▼ IT Problem Management
  Gary Walker

▼ Data Warehousing: Architecture and Implementation
  Mark Humphries, Michael W. Hawkins, Michelle C. Dy

▼ Software Development: Building Reliable Systems
  Marc Hamilton

▼ IT Automation: The Quest for Lights Out
  Howie Lyke with Debra Cottone

▼ IT Organization: Building a Worldclass Infrastructure
  Harris Kern, Stuart D. Galup, Guy Nemiro

▼ High Availability: Design, Techniques, and Processes
  Michael Hawkins, Floyd Piedad

▼ IT Services: Costs, Metrics, Benchmarking, and Marketing
  Anthony F. Tardugno, Thomas R. DiPasquale, Robert E. Matthews

HARRIS KERN'S ENTERPRISE COMPUTING INSTITUTE

IT Problem Management

Gary Walker

Prentice Hall PTR
Upper Saddle River, NJ 07458
www.phptr.com

Library of Congress Cataloging-in-Publication Data

Walker, Gary (Gary S.)
    IT problem management / by Gary Walker
      p. cm.
    Includes index.
    ISBN 0-13-030770-X
     1. Electronic data processing--Management. 2. Information technology. I. Title.

    QA76.9.M3 W35 2001
    004'.068--dc21
                                           2001016383

Editorial/production supervision: *Vincent Janoski*
Acquisitions editor: *Greg Doench*
Marketing manager: *Debby vanDijk*
Manufacturing manager: *Alexis Heydt*
Cover design director: *Jerry Votta*
Series design: *Gail Cocker-Bogusz*

© 2001 by Prentice-Hall

Published by Prentice Hall PTR
Prentice-Hall, Inc.
Upper Saddle River, NJ 07458

Prentice Hall books are widely used by corporations and government agencies
for training, marketing, and resale.

The publisher offers discounts on this book when ordered in bulk quantities.
For more information, contact: Corporate Sales Department, Phone: 800-382-3419;
Fax: 201-236-7141; E-mail: corpsales@prenhall.com; or write: Prentice Hall PTR,
Corp. Sales Dept., One Lake Street, Upper Saddle River, NJ 07458.

Printed in the United States of America
10 9 8 7 6 5 4 3 2 1

ISBN   0-13-030770-X

Prentice-Hall International (UK) Limited, *London*
Prentice-Hall of Australia Pty. Limited, *Sydney*
Prentice-Hall Canada Inc., *Toronto*
Prentice-Hall Hispanoamericana, S.A., *Mexico*
Prentice-Hall of India Private Limited, *New Delhi*
Prentice-Hall of Japan, Inc., *Tokyo*
Prentice-Hall Asia Pte. Ltd.
Editora Prentice-Hall do Brasil, Ltda., *Rio de Janeiro*

To Sharon—you are truly magnificent.

Contents

Chapter 10

Service Level Agreements   175

Chapter 11

Service Center Tools   181

Chapter 12

Motivation   209

Index   229

Acknowledgments

Special thanks to the following people for their insights, expertise, and contributions. They have developed, redeveloped, managed, and are still managing service centers, and they understand what it takes to build and run a world-class service center. Their hard work has benefited all of us.

To Wayne Markover and Anthony Tuorto for taking me into the trenches and sharing their expertise during the hectic D2k upgrade and service center upgrade. I couldn't have done this without them (and they're not bad, guys either)! See you in Montana.

To Harris Kern for the insight, opportunity, and friendship. I look forward to a future journey.

To Tom Shumacher, consultant extraordinaire, who just completed the rebuilding and retooling of a huge service center, where broadcast is king and downtime is unacceptable. I suppose those 10,000 external customers and the millions of people who rely on the information they receive are pretty important too.

To Stephanie Jason for sharing her expertise and taking the time to tell me about her past and present help desks and the plans for the future.

To Alan Dettmering and George Saulnier. They have recently built and are now operating one of the finest service centers around. Their unique approach to tier 1 staffing has been successful and could be the model for the future. Who would have guessed that tier 2 resources would consider it desirable to make it to tier 1? I hear they have a fantastic resource-loading model that they might be willing to share.

Preface

In the past three decades, businesses have made staggering investments in technology to increase their productivity and efficiency. The technological infrastructure of these companies has become increasingly sophisticated and complex. Most companies today are extremely dependent on their technological infrastructure. Operating without it is like trying to run a business without a telephone or electricity. Businesses depend on their technology at least as much as, perhaps more than, any other utility. However, unlike the telephone and electric industries, technology has not had the benefit of 100 + years to mature under the control of a handful of companies. Thousands of companies contribute to technology, each doing whatever they think will sell the best. Extreme and rapid innovation is the rule, not the exception. Change is the rule, not the exception. The resulting complexity has posed a new challenge for companies: how to realize the potential and anticipated benefits of the investments in an environment of constant change.

Businesses are so reliant on technology that they need it to operate as reliably, consistently, and universally as the telephone and electricity. We are a long way from achieving that level of service. Businesses face rising costs because of constant failures that result in lost productivity. It is very difficult and expensive to find the resources with the expertise to manage and repair their infrastructures. It is extremely difficult and expensive to keep those resources trained to manage a constantly evolving environment.

But guess what. There is no choice but to invest in technology, because it has to be done. Business cannot stop investing in technology or they will be crushed by the competition. So what have they done? They have standardized to limit the diversity, the expertise required, and the problems associated with diversity. They have striven to make the infrastructure as reliable as the telephone and to keep employees productive. And they have created a team that has the skills, the facilities, and the charter to fix existing problems and reduce future problems. That team is the service center, and this book shares how the best of those teams are doing just that.

Technology impacts more than just a business's internal operations. What about the company's customers? They often need support, as well. More companies are realizing the value of providing quality service to its customers. Some studies have indicated that keeping a customer costs one-tenth the price of getting a new one, while the return business from satisfied customers count for substantially more than one-tenth of a company's revenue. It makes good economic sense to spend money on keeping existing clients satisfied. For many companies, that means providing customers with quality support for the products and services they purchase. So who in the company provides that service? You guessed it—the service center.

What is a service center? It is an organization whose charter and mission are to provide support services to internal or external customers, or to both. It is a concentration of expertise, processes, and tools dedicated to taking customers' requests and fulfilling them in a timely and cost-effective manner, leaving the customer delighted with the experience. A service center has a defined range of service offerings, from fixing problems to providing value-added services, and everything in between.

This book is intended to help a company set up that service center and deliver those services cost effectively. The book focuses on structuring the organization and building the processes to move service requests efficiently and effectively through the organization to deliver quality service to the customer. It discusses the pitfalls that afflict many service centers and offers techniques and solutions to avoid those pitfalls. The book discusses the tools available to help a service center manage its business and deliver high quality cost-effective services to customers.

The traditional help desk is still around, but many have evolved into service centers. As more businesses are faced with increasing technology costs and increasing pressure to be productive and efficient internally—while delighting external customers—many more help desks will be forced to evolve. For a well-run help desk, the evolution is natural and not overly difficult.

Most help desks were originally designed to provide one type of service, technical support. Help desks traditionally helped customers by fixing their problems and answering their questions. The help desk concentrated technical expertise, problem management processes, and tools to track and resolve customer problems, answer customer questions, and deliver that support as cost effectively as possible. Many help desks have done this quite successfully, and many have not. As their companies reengineer and look to streamline operations, many company executives have asked the simple question, "Today, you provide one type of service—technical support. How hard would it be to add additional services?" It's a fair question, because the help desk already takes service requests, tracks them, makes delivery commitments to customers, delivers the services, and charges the customers. The organization, the processes, the tools are in place.

The evolution usually starts small, with simple, technology–related, value-added services, such as ordering PCs. You need a PC, contact the help desk. They'll figure out what you need, order it, track the order, install it when it arrives, and then support you if you have any questions. Voila, the help desk is now providing value-added services. Since you are ordering the equipment and maintaining and fixing it all the time, how about keeping track of it? No one else does. Again, voila, you're providing a value-added asset management service. Since you have all of that valuable information, can you report on it quarterly to the insurance and risk anagement department and the finance and accounting group? Yep, another-value added service. Hey, you guys are pretty good at this stuff. We need computer training. Can you make arrangements for that and then handle the scheduling? Its happened. You are no longer just a help desk—you are a service center, offering both traditional help desk support and value-added services to your customers.

This goes along for a while, and you tweak the processes and improve your delivery capability. Then, someone in the company gets the idea that a single point of contact for many internal services would be handy, and since you're already capable of handling value-added services and you do it so well, you should consider handling many more. That certainly sounds reasonable. For example, how about a service for new employees. Instead of the HR department contacting the telecom department, the help desk, and the facilities department every time a new employee is hired, why don't they just contact the service center and let them coordinate the rest. Like magic, you've added a service called New Employee Setup, or maybe even better, Amaze the New Employee.

You gather the vital information—her name, who she works for, when she starts, what budget to charge, where she'll be sitting. You order her PC, you contact telecom to set up her phone and voice mailbox, and you contact facilities to set up her workspace. Then, you notify security and set up her appointment to get a badge, you schedule her into the next orientation class, and you schedule her in the next "PC and Networking in Our Company" class. Finally, you generate the standard welcome-on-board letter that tells her the classes she is scheduled for and where they are located. You have standard attachments that explain how to use the phone and how to log on to the PC, and most importantly, how to reach the service center. You email the package to HR, who is merely awaiting her arrival, secure in the knowledge that all is well, everything is ready, and that the new employee will be duly impressed with her new company.

Just as you do with the problems you handle, you follow up on this service to make sure the work is done on time. Now your follow-up includes telecom and facilities, who essentially act like any other tier 2 group. Instead of generating a trouble ticket, you generate a tracking ticket, which is associated with another new type of ticket, a work order. One work order is sent to telecom and another to facilities. The new tracking ticket looks amazingly similar to a trouble ticket. It has the same contact information—the customer name and location, the desired delivery date, the name of the agent who took the order, when the order was placed, the current status, and who else is involved. Work order tickets really aren't much different than a traditional trouble ticket to dispatch, for example, a hardware support technician that includes information on where to go, what needs to be done, when it needs to be done, who is handling it, its current status and priority, and so on. The work order ticket even goes into a queue, just like a problem ticket dispatched to any tier 2 support group. And just as with trouble tickets, you have processes and tools in place to escalate the tracking and work order tickets, and to send notifications if there is a problem or if more work to be done.

The entire process is, logically, very similar to managing problems. The information must be tracked, people are assigned to do the work, the work is prioritized, time commitments are in place, processes are in place to handle work that can't be done in the agreed upon time frame, additional levels of expertise are available to handle difficulties. Perhaps most importantly, it is all initiated, tracked, and closed centrally.

Many help desks resist this evolution. If their house is not in order and they are struggling to handle technical support, they should resist. Get the technical support in order first. Work on your problem management processes and take advantage of your existing tools. When your problem management processes are working, they'll work just as well for other value-added services. That is the secret. If you can make and meet time commitmentsfor technical support to customers, you can easily add new value-added services to your repertoire. Value-added services are like the simplest, most common, recurring problems your customers call about. They're easy because the request is common, so everyone is familiar with it. The solution is known; its predefined. Processes to deliver the solution are already in place. Processes to deal with unexpected complications are already defined and in use. Simple. You have the tools, the people, the processes, the organization, and the experience.

▶ Overview

This book was written because problem management is one of the most important processes for any IT organization. Yet, of the hundreds of companies we have worked with, it is most often not done well. It seems that many companies consider problem management only as an afterthought, a necessary evil, overhead, or worse, all of the above.

So what is problem management? Problem management is a formal set of processes designed and implemented to quickly and efficiently resolve problems and questions. Those problems and questions come from customers, both internal and external.

Why is problem management important? Because how well you do at resolving those problems and questions determines how your customers perceive you. Further, how you provide those services can make an enormous difference in your overall costs—not only your costs, but also the costs your customers incur.

Do a poor job on your problem management processes and your customers will think ill of you. Internal customers can be the most vicious, because they know who to complain to. They also complain to each other, and before you know it, the entire company believes you to be incompetent, at least as far as problem management goes. Worse, that attitude can easily fail over to the entire IT department. Let's face it—most of the IT department's exposure is through the problem management function (the help desk) and that is where your reputation will be made or broken. It isn't hard to justify spending to improve problem management when you calculate the number of hours of internal downtime and the average cost per hour the company absorbs for that downtime. Run the numbers and see for yourself.

External customers can be less vicious on a personal level, but from the business perspective, their impression is even more important. If they don't like the way you handle problems, they may complain, but worse, they will most certainly vote with their dollar by taking it elsewhere—and will probably tell everyone they know to do the same. Your company worked hard and spent significant dollars to win that customer. To lose them because you provided poor service is an enormous waste. What will it cost you to win them back? Can you win them back? Can you ever win their friends and associates? Many studies have found that it is much cheaper to keep a customer than to win a new one. If your company hasn't seen this light yet, you need to convince them.

This book was written to tell you what you can and should consider doing to improve your problem management processes. It is based on experience gained at many different sites and focuses on improving service delivery and efficiency. It's true—you can do it better and cheaper. You may have to spend some capital up front, but a standard project cost/benefit analysis will show that you can recoup those costs quickly, and in some cases, can generate significant dollars.

This book was written for CIOs, vice presidents, help desk and service center managers, and the senior-level internal customers of the problem management department—anyone who can influence the problem management function and wants to understand more about what can and should be done to improve performance.

I appreciate any feedback you wish to provide. You can reach me at either *garywalker@home.com* or *xogsw@hotmail.com*.

Best of luck to you.

Gary Walker

Introduction to Problem Management

Problem management is a business function comprised of people, processes, and tools organized and chartered to resolve customer problems. This function has traditionally been the responsibility of and managed by the help desk. As companies have drastically increased spending on technology, the visibility of the help desk and the pressure on it to perform have increased dramatically as well. The complexity of so much new technology and the rapid distribution of it into the customer environment has made the once straightforward job of the help desk very difficult. The breadth and depth of expertise now required to support a common infrastructure is practically unimaginable compared to the mainframe environment of the 1970s and 1980s. It has become more difficult to support external customers as well, because of the complexity of their environments and the "standard" services they so often demand. Most customers expect "on-demand" services with a variety of access options to those services—telephone, Internet, email, and more. If you can't provide these services, customers will take their business to someone who can.

▶ 1.1 Help Desk

The help desk is chartered to help customers use products and services. The help desk has expert resources available to solve problems that customers encounter when using those products and services. The help desk's customers can be the company's customers who buy the company's products and services, or they can be company employees who use other vendors' products and services to do their jobs. Armed with good communication skills, technical skills, problem-solving skills, and tools of the trade, help desk employees identify, track, and resolve customer problems.

Many help desks have evolved to offer services beyond the traditional problem-solving and product usage services and now offer additional value-added services. It is a natural evolution that an organization that has the people, the processes, the structure, and the tools to handle one type of service add additional services. Throughout *IT Problem Management,* I'll refer to this new organization as a *service center.* A service center offers its customers various services, including traditional technical and problem support, as well as value-added services such as ordering PCs, coordinating and overseeing work orders to set up new employees or to move an employee to a new office, taking orders for company products, and coordinating referrals. The list goes on and on.

The process that the service center implements to manage the delivery of these services is referred to as the *problem management processes* in this book. The terminology is not intended to imply that the process is applicable only to the technical support or problem support services of the service center. These processes are in place to handle all services offered by the service center and are capable of handling any problems associated with delivering those services. If you want to, think of them as service management processes. As described in this book, the processes have elements and steps that are unique to solving problems. But many of the components, such as receiving the request, validating the request, logging it, and routing it to the person best suited to handle it, apply whether the request is to solve a problem or buy a PC. Further, the structure of the organization and the mechanisms in place to prioritize, make service commitments, provide follow-up, and measure performance apply to any type of service provisioning.

1.2 Internal and External Service Centers

A service center can have internal or external customers, or both. Internal customers are employees who work for the company that sponsors the service center. External customers are those who purchase products or services (or both) from the company. A service center that supports external customers helps those customers use the products or services they purchased from the company. The service center may even sell them additional products and services. A service center that supports internal customers helps company employees use the internal infrastructure the company has put in place to help them do their jobs. Many companies have one service center that focuses on supporting internal customers and a second service center that focuses on supporting external customers. Why would a company do that? Since both are set up with essentially the same processes, the same structure, the same kinds of prioritization and escalation, why not combine them and get the economies of scale?

That is a valid question that deserves close consideration. While there are many similarities, there are also many differences. Perhaps foremost, the external service center is generally a profit center, while the internal service center usually is not. This means that the reporting requirements are different and the solicitation of funding is different. In most cases, the way each center bills its clients is different. Internal service centers often distribute charges, while the external service center generates invoices. The types of contracts that the service centers enter into with their clients is also different, at least in terms of the binding implications.

From an operational perspective, internal service centers usually have to support a much broader range of products and services than an external service center. This is the case when the internal service center must support the wide variety of products and services in use across the entire corporate infrastructure, while the external service center supports only the products and services the company sells. Even if the number of products and services the company sells is as broad as the number of products and services the company uses in-house, they are most likely different products and services, requiring completely different skill sets. Even Microsoft has an internal service center and a separate external service center, despite the significant overlap in the products they sell and the products they use in-house.

▶ 1.3 Building a Successful Service Center

1.3.1 Defining the Mission

The primary purpose of all service centers, both internal and external, is service delivery. Your service delivery goals, the services you will provide, the service levels you will offer, and whether you will be a profit center or cost center must be determined, documented, and understood at the outset of establishing the service center. You need a mission statement that summarizes your charter. Your mission statement very broadly defines what you are supposed to do and establishes the overall expectation of how well you will do it. Establishing a service center is first a higher management decision, the expectations of which may or may not be realistic. You must be prepared to negotiate the feasibility of each goal. Be careful with words like *most* when stating expectations. Does *most* mean 60 percent or 90 percent? The difference between solving 60 percent of all problems in 2 hours or less and 90 percent of all problems in 2 hours or less is immense. It's comparable to the difference between 99.9 percent reliability (8.76 hours of downtime per year) and 99.99999 percent reliability (4 seconds of downtime per year). Both are doable, but the difference in costs is enormous.

A clearly defined mission statement helps to ensure that everyone is working to achieve the same goals and defines the expectations of both management and customers. Those expectations are how you and the service center will be measured. A sample mission statement is: "To increase customer productivity by promptly resolving problems, identifying and eliminating the cause of problems, and delivering other value-added services as required."

1.3.2 Defining the Service Statement

The mission statement is very broad. Too broad, in fact, to establish the scope of what you will really be responsible for doing. The scope of your services establishes the bounds of the service center. If the bounds are not clear from the mission statement, then you can clarify it now, in a service statement, or catalog. The service catalog establishes the scope of the services you will provide and should eventually contain a complete listing of those services. The list further clarifies what you will *not* do. The better you define your services, the clearer it is to your management, customers, and staff what you do.

This list is the basis you use to determine how to structure the organization to deliver the services and what types of tools and resources you need. You could, and probably should, define service levels for each service offered. Once you have done that, you can use this list to create service level agreements and service contracts with your customers. Negotiating these agreements may lead to modifying your service levels.

The list of services is also the basis for defining responsibility within the service center. For each service, you must define who will be responsible for delivering the service. This responsibility matrix allows you to create pools of resources that are best suited to deliver groups of services that require related skills.

When you have defined the list of services that you will provide, the service levels you want to provide, the skills you need to deliver the services, and an idea of the volume of requests for the services, you can begin to design your organization structure.

Based on the breadth of services you provide and the breadth of skills required to handle requests for those services, you can determine how to best organize your resources to field specific calls. Many service centers create pools of resources with common skills to deliver subsets of their services. This accommodates the incredible variety of products that most service centers support. Based on the complexity of the environment (products and services) you support, you can determine the tiers of support required to handle requests.

Two important characteristics of service delivery must be considered when setting up the organization structure, creating the problem management processes, and selecting support tools. They are the *service delivery type* and the *service delivery mode*. Together, they establish your service delivery model. The service delivery types are *immediate* and *managed,* and the service delivery modes are *reactive* and *proactive.* The delivery type is critical for determining staffing.

The immediate type means that you provide services on-demand in a first in/first out approach. It is the most typical delivery type and is characterized by telephone support. The customer calls and is placed in a queue; calls are taken in the order in which they are received, and when his or her turn comes, the customer is transferred to the next available agent, who proceeds to deliver the service immediately.

The managed delivery type allows for better balancing and prioritizing of requests because the customer has no expectation of immediate service delivery. Managed service requests come into the service center, typically as an electronic request, and then the service center reviews and assigns the requests as it deems most appropriate. This includes scheduling the delivery of the service to balance the ratio of requests to agents.

Most service centers offer both immediate and managed service delivery. There will almost always be a requirement to provide immediate service delivery and it is the most commonly used type. However, more and more service centers have augmented that type with the managed type in an effort to better balance resource loading by distributing requests throughout the day. The more requests you can handle using the managed delivery approach, the better you will be able to balance your workload and staffing levels.

The reactive and proactive modes reflect your approach to problem solving. Many service centers were traditionally 100 percent reactive. Agents were available and waiting for customers to call in for support. While you must still have agents available to react to immediate requests, many service centers have become much more proactive in their problem-solving approach. Being proactive means looking for, finding, and resolving problems or conditions that will cause problems before they impact the customer. To do this, service center agents must test hardware, software, and communications for problems that their customers might encounter. They must establish acceptable performance and capacity thresholds for infrastructure components and then use monitoring tools to detect when those thresholds have been crossed. Based on the findings, the service center initiates improvement projects to fix those items before they impact the customer. The service center is also proactive in telling customers about known problems and providing solutions or workarounds for those problems before the customer has experienced them. When a customer knows about a problem in advance, he or she either avoids it or experiences it and has a workaround in hand. Some customers will call no matter what, but at least some won't, which means you have proactively eliminated requests.

After you've identified your mission, the services you will provide, your service delivery goals, and a structure in which to provide the services, you can develop processes to pull it all together to operate smoothly.

▶ 1.4 Problem Management Process Overview

Problem management is a complex process. Many organizations have been providing services via a formal service center for years. As time has passed, those service centers have improved in all aspects of providing services. These improvements have come in the form of process improvement, performance improvements, cost improvements, and improved efficiencies. Service centers have also established beyond the shadow of a doubt that they can have either a very positive or a very negative impact on their company's bottom line. Service centers have driven the support industry such that today's support tools are far superior to those that were available just five years ago. Much like computer hardware technology, these processes and tools continue to evolve at a breakneck pace.

We will examine the problem management process by dividing it into five core processes, as shown in Figure 1–1. The core processes are

- problem identification
- customer validation
- problem logging
- service delivery
- knowledge capture and sharing

Further along in the book, we will review each of these core problem management processes in detail and will decompose them into subprocesses and identify important considerations. At the highest level, service requests and problems are brought to the attention of the service center; the service center validates both the customer and the requested service, logs the request, takes action to deliver the required service, and then captures and shares any new information about the transaction that may be of use the next time a similar request is fielded. It's as simple as that at the high level. When it's all said and done, management reviews the process to see how well it was done and how it could be improved.

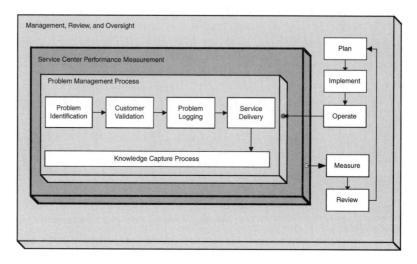

Figure 1–1 Problem management process: high level.

1.4.1 Problem Identification

Problem identification is the people, processes, and tools used to detect and report problems. Problems can be detected before or after they occur (proactively or reactively). Problems are detected by monitoring tools, by IT staff, and by customers. The goal is to detect as many problems as possible before they occur so that they can be fixed before the customer has to endure a productivity-killing problem. A variety of testing and monitoring tools are available to aid in proactive detection and are discussed in Chapter 11, "Service Center Tools." Problems can also be detected in advance through trend analysis and observation. No matter how many tools and techniques are employed, we will never be able to detect all the problems proactively, so customers will always be a primary source of problem detection.

Whether a problem is detected before or after it occurs, access methods must be put in place that allow the problems to be easily reported to the service center. Those same access methods will be used to allow customers to request value-added services. Most service centers employ multiple access methods for the reporting of detected problems. They include the telephone, electronic methods such as email or a Web gateway, person-to-person reporting, tool-to-tool automatic reporting (monitoring tool-to-problem management system), and facsimile.

1.4.2 Customer Validation

Once a problem has been reported, or when a customer has a value-added request, the service center must validate both the customer and the service request. The service center has three tasks in this regard. First, the center must validate that the customer is a valid customer. This is an important step for internal and external service centers. The center must next validate that the service requested is a service that the center provides. If not, the center may refer the customer elsewhere. Finally, if the customer is a valid customer and the request is a valid service, the center must check to see if the customer is eligible to receive the requested service.

It used to be that only external service centers performed validation. This made sense because they were generally charging customers for support. However, it is becoming increasingly important for internal service centers to validate customers and services as well. Because so many businesses rely on their technical infrastructure and have so much company information online, security considerations demand the validation process.

1.4.3 Problem Logging

Problem logging occurs after a problem has been detected and validated. As discussed, the logging process applies to any valid service the center provides, not just to problems. Once a valid request has been received and validated, a record of the request must be captured. This record, or ticket, is the basic document used to manage the request from start to finish. It is the service center's record of the transaction and is used not only to get the work done but to generate performance measurements. Two important facts must be captured during the logging process: the request priority and the request category. The priority determines the service delivery timeframe, that is, when the work should be completed. Based on the priority, the service center assigns resources to complete the work within the predefined timeframe. The category assigned to the ticket determines handling and routing, if routing is necessary. If, for example, the request is to fix a hardware problem, correctly categorizing the request will ensure that the request is routed to the resource pool that handles hardware problems. Categorizing is a critical step because incorrectly categorized requests can be routed to the wrong resource pools, which introduces delays in service delivery and could cause the service center to miss its delivery time commitments. Further, the categories are used to gather metrics that allow you to evaluate the type and volume of requests coming into the service center.

1.4.4 Service Delivery

Service delivery is the process of actually doing the work required to complete the request and deliver the results to the customer. The key to service delivery is the category and priority assigned to the request. If the request is for a value-added service, the work is most often done by someone other than the agent who logged the request. For example, if the request is to order a PC, the agent who logs the request has no more work to do on that request. Depending on the systems you have in place, work orders may be generated and routed automatically when the agent selects the "Order PC" service. For technical support requests, the agent logging the request is usually the first person to attempt delivery. As with the "Order PC" service, the agent may immediately route the request, depending on the particular request, such as a request to fix hardware.

The important aspect of service delivery is to deliver the requested service in the predetermined timeframe as cost-effectively as possible. How this is done depends on how the organization is structured. In a multipool, multitier environment, procedures must be in place to handle escalation and priorities. For technical support requests, procedures must be in place to ensure that problems are resolved quickly and consistently. A detailed discussion of these procedures for each tier in a multitier environment is included in Chapter 7, "Service Delivery."

1.4.5 Knowledge Capture and Sharing Process

The knowledge capture and sharing process is in place to aid in the delivery of technical support requests. This process is intended to gather and share the collective knowledge of service center agents—the *institutional knowledge*. When an agent identifies a new problem and a solution, or workaround, this process creates a record of that problem and solution, referred to as a *knowledge base report*. The report is then made available to all other agents. If a similar problem is reported, the agent can search for and retrieve the knowledge base report. This eliminates the need for the agent to take the time to solve a problem that someone else has already solved and documented.

All common, recurring problems should have an associated knowledge base report that details the service center's approved solution or workaround. When technical support requests arrive at the service center, agents should immediately search the knowledge base for the standard resolution. There are three benefits to this approach. First, the agent doesn't waste time troubleshooting problems that have already been resolved. Second, all agents will apply the service center's standard solution for the given problem, which increases consistency. Finally, new workarounds and solutions are communicated to all agents via the knowledge base, and then applied consistently.

The knowledge capture and sharing process is discussed in detail in Chapter 8, "Knowledge Capture and Sharing." Knowledge base tools are discussed in Chapter 11.

▶ 1.5 Management Review and Oversight

The service center is a clearinghouse for both problems and requested services. In this role, the service center is in a unique position to gather data about problems with the internal infrastructure as well as problems that customers encounter while using the products and services the company sells. The service center is also in a unique position to gather intelligence about what customers, both internal and external, want in terms of services and product enhancements. This is incredibly valuable strategic information about the company's product and service offerings. The data is also extremely valuable to internal operations because it points out recurring problems with the internal infrastructure so that improvement projects can be initiated to eliminate productivity-killing problems.

Management review must also focus internally, that is, on the service center's performance. This critical process must constantly review and improve the problem management processes, the staff, the tools, and the structure of the organization. The objective is to continually improve performance, "raising the bar" year after year. A complete discussion of the metrics that service center management should review is given in Chapter 9, "Management, Review, and Oversight."

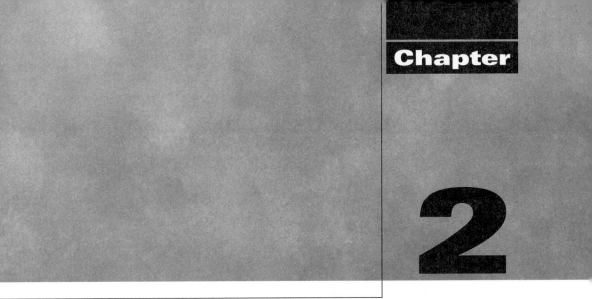

Service Center Organization

If you have the luxury of organizing or reorganizing your service center, there are a number of important factors to consider. Certainly among the most important of these is the type of service center you plan to run. It is important to consider whether you will provide the absolute best service available or the minimum service required to get by. You must determine the environment you are currently supporting and the environment you plan to support in the future. You must also consider the expected call volume and call complexity. Based on the volume and complexity of calls, you can use queuing theory to determine the number of resources and the technical skills you require to handle the anticipated volume and complexity. Another important consideration in organizing a service center is the types of support tools you will need. The tools you deploy to support the service center are likely to affect both the number of resources you require and the model you use to organize the resources.

Based on these factors, there are various approaches you can use to maximize the utilization of resources to meet your service levels and objectives. As noted in Chapter 1, "Introduction to Problem Management," these approaches are referred to as the *service delivery type*. The two service delivery types are *immediate* and *managed*. In the immediate model, customers go into a queue and wait for the next available agent, who immediately works with the customer to resolve the problem. In the managed model, the customer typically sends an email or fax, or fills out a Web-based form, which then goes into a queue. Unlike the immediate model, the managed model usually involves a controller (manual or automated) that reviews, prioritizes, and then assigns the ticket to an agent or an agent pool. Today, many service centers use both of these models.

There are, of course, various ways of implementing these models to maximize the utilization of your resources. You may implement one or more tiers of support to optimize the provision of service to customers and to optimize your utilization of resources.

▶ 2.1 Immediate Response Model

Implementing the immediate response model means that you will attempt to handle calls (or walk-ups) when they arrive. Customers will contact the service center using the contact methods you have provided for them. These methods can include the telephone, a line to stand in, email, fax, chat room, etc. Once customers have contacted the service center, you must have some mechanism for routing them to the next available agent or engineer or service representative. The routing mechanism can be as simple as one line for each agent, or it can be a sophisticated call tree that routes the customer to the most appropriate queue based on customer input; the customer then waits for the next available agent in that queue. There are other routing options in between. For example, if you do not have a call distribution system, one or more receptionists can take calls and then manually route (dispatch) them to the appropriate person or queue in the next tier.

In this model, the customer contacts the service center and is then routed to the next available agent. The pool, or pools, of agents that provide immediate response are in tier 1. Tier 1 can be one pool of agents or it can be multiple pools of agents. The simplest organizational model for a service center consists of one tier with one pool of resources. Queuing theory states that this would be the most efficient model for handling call volume while maximizing resource utilization. This model ignores complexity and variability, however, because it assumes that each resource in the pool can handle any issue that comes in. This may or may not be possible in the environment you support. In environments that support multiple products from multiple vendors on various platforms, it is not reasonable to expect that any one person can handle every type of call. Even if you could find a pool of gurus capable of providing that level of support, it would be more expensive and less efficient to use those expensive resources to handle common, recurring, simple problems.

Two examples of the single-tier, immediate response service center model are shown in Figure 2–1.

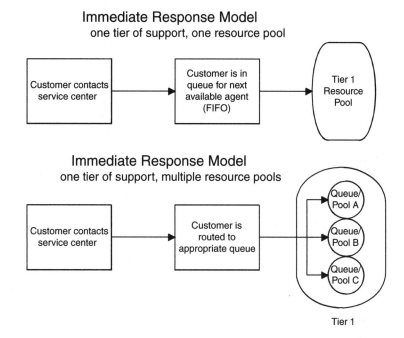

Figure 2–1 Single-tier, immediate response service center models.

In the second example, tier 1 support is subdivided into multiple pools. As mentioned above, queuing theory states that multiple pools are less efficient than a single pool. This makes logical sense, since resources in pool A and C may be underutilized, while all resources in pool B may be occupied and have many customers waiting in the queue. This does not mean that subdividing tier 1 resources into multiple pools is a bad idea. Suppose you provide support for multiple products from multiple vendors and you receive a significant number of calls from customers each day. It may be unreasonable to expect that each person can handle any call about any product, so you could divide your resources into pools that specialize in one or more products or one or more types of problems. When customers contact the service center, they are routed to the queue that is best suited to address their issue.

There are three factors you need to consider when designing the number of tiers you require and how to organize each of those tiers (one or more pools). The factors are call variability, call complexity, and call volume. Call variability refers to the different types of requests that come into the service center. The more types of requests received, the higher the variability. Request variability is important to understand because it indicates the amount of knowledge required to handle the requests. In a multiproduct, multivendor, multiplatform environment, the variability is high. If you support a highly standardized environment with few products, the variability is low. The higher the variability, the more knowledge required to provide support. The lower the variability, the less total support knowledge required.

2.1.1 Request Variability

Based on the variability of your workload, you can decide how to organize the support tier. In Figure 2–1, tier 1 is subdivided into three resource pools. This indicates that variability of requests was high enough that one resource could not be expected to efficiently handle all types of requests coming into the service center. For example, pool A may handle all requests that deal with desktop productivity software, such as Microsoft Office and Microsoft Windows. Pool B may handle all requests that deal with internal corporate applications, such as the general ledger and human resource systems. Pool C may handle all value-added services, such as ordering PCs, moves, and training requests. Keep in mind that by subdividing resource pools, you are potentially reducing efficiency in handling the call volume, because pool A may be overwhelmed with calls, while pool B and pool C have excess capacity.

One approach to deal with this inefficiency is to allow calls to overflow from one pool to another, as shown in Figure 2–2.

For this overflow approach to work, the resources in pool B must have at least some capability of dealing with requests that are typically handled by pool A. That can occur as a result of cross-training as well as having access to a shared knowledge base.

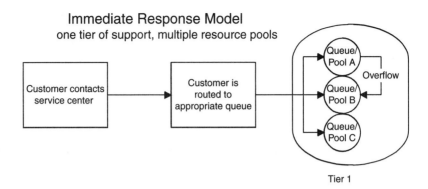

Figure 2–2 The overflow approach to handling call volume.

Several points to keep in mind are

- The fewer pools within a tier, the better in terms of your ability to handle call volume efficiently.
- The fewer the pools within a tier, the broader the knowledge required by the staff.
- Cross-training pools within a tier allows for more effective call overflow.

2.1.2 Request Complexity

So far, we have considered the variability of the requests but we haven't considered the request volume or complexity. The volume and complexity of requests play an equally important role in determining how to structure the service center organization. Ideally, a service center (and its customers) would like to handle all requests immediately. However, when you consider the volume and complexity of requests, this may not be possible.

Complexity refers to the level of difficulty encountered while servicing the request. Many requests are recurrent and are thus well defined and well known by the staff. These requests are not difficult to service and therefore have a low complexity. Other requests occur infrequently and require more research. These may involve interaction between multiple products, rarely used functions and features, and so on. Complex issues usually take more time to resolve and may require more technical expertise than is available in the tier 1 resource pool.

The complexity of requests should be used to determine the number of tiers of support you require. Thus far we have only considered one tier of support, which may or may not be appropriate, depending on the complexity of the requests you receive. If a significant portion, say 90 percent, of the requests you receive are complex, then one tier of support would be appropriate. The tier would be staffed with highly skilled specialists who could handle the complex requests. They would be organized into multiple pools within the tier, based on their expertise. The staffing levels would have to take into consideration the volume of requests and the additional time required to handle complex requests. The same staff could also handle the 10 percent of calls that are less complex.

If on the other hand, 90 percent of the calls are routine, noncomplex calls, an additional tier of support should be considered. The additional tier, tier 2 in this case, would handle the 10 percent of calls that are too complex or too time consuming to be handled by the tier 1 resources. The diagram in Figure 2–3 illustrates a two-tier response model.

As illustrated in the diagram, there are two tiers of support. In this example, 90 percent of the calls are not complex and are handled by generalists in tier 1. However, when a tier 1 agent encounters a request that he or she cannot resolve, the request can be routed, or escalated, to the appropriate tier 2 group. In the example, pool A is responsible for desktop productivity software and the desktop operating system, and routes calls when necessary to pool 1. Let's assume there are 10 agents in pool A and they handle 92 percent of the requests that are routed to them. Generally, the tier 2 pools have fewer agents than tier 1 because they are handling far fewer requests—only 8 percent of the total in this case. Keep in mind that even though they are handling fewer requests, the requests they are handling are more complex and will generally take longer to resolve. An evaluation of your resolution times by tier will bear this out.

As with tier 1, the variability of expertise required will help you determine how many pools of expertise are needed in tier 2. In Figure 2–3, pool B in tier 1 can escalate calls to three different pools in tier 2. This is because of the variability of the expertise required to handle complex requests across the various corporate applications that pool B supports. Pool 2 in tier 2 may handle all complex requests for corporate financial systems, while pool 3 handles all complex requests for the human resource systems.

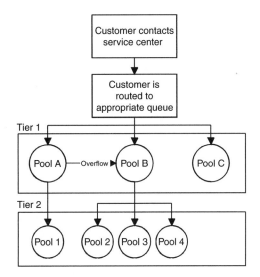

Two-Tier Multipool Model

Figure 2–3 Two-tier response model for high-volume, routine calls.

Notice that pool C in tier 1 does not require a second tier of support, because they are capable of handling all requests in their area of responsibility.

The multitiered model is a good structure for efficiently utilizing technical expertise when the bulk of the requests you handle are not complex. In most tiered service centers, each successive tier has more specialized technical expertise than the preceding tier. Generally speaking, the more specialized the expertise, the more expensive the resource. This means that the generalists in tier one are on average less expensive than the tier 2 specialists. The multitier model is efficient because the less expensive resources are handling more requests, thus reducing your costs for servicing requests. You would not want a $70,000-a-year Microsoft Certified Systems Engineer (MCSE) answering questions about formatting Word documents when a $25,000-a-year generalist could provide the same service.

The multitiered model is also useful for handling overflow from tier 1. If pool A is overwhelmed with requests, their overflow can be routed to pool 1 in tier 2. This should be the exception rather than the rule, because pool 1 has their own work to do and as mentioned above, it may not be the most efficient use of tier 2 expertise. If you use this overflow approach, keep track of how often it occurs. If it occurs frequently, you should add additional resources to the tier 1 pool. It should be fairly easy to justify the costs of the additional resources if your tier 2 resources are indeed more expensive than tier 1.

There are several disadvantages to using a multitiered model. A multitiered organization is more difficult to manage and requires additional layers of management and overhead expenses. While tier 1 may have shift managers in charge of the entire tier 1 staff during the shift, each tier 2 and tier 3 pool may also have a manager, particularly if the resources in the pool are not dedicated to the service center. Processes must be put in place to handle the movement of requests between pools and between tiers. Those processes must be developed, trained, implemented, and maintained. Customer requests take longer to resolve as the request moves from tier to tier, because they are generally moved into a new waiting queue. Customers usually have to explain their request again and answer additional questions every time their request is moved to a new tier. Finally, the multitiered model can foster morale problems, because it often creates a class system, which closely matches tier level. Tier 1 resources can be viewed as lower class service center employees because they have less expertise than tier 2 resources and are generally paid less.

2.1.3 Request Volume

The same principle applies to complexity. When you use request complexity as a gauge for determining the need for a second tier of support, you must consider the volume of complex requests. If nearly all of your requests are simple and can be handled by tier 1 resources, then it probably does not make sense to add a second tier of support. As mentioned above, adding a second tier of support adds complexity and additional overhead to the service center. It also adds delays into the resolution time. In this scenario, it may be better to add several more highly trained resources to the tier 1 pool. These resources would take requests just like everyone else, but would also be available if less skilled agents needed to redirect requests that were beyond their capabilities. A second approach in this scenario is to have the more skilled agents available as mentors to everyone else in the resource pool. As mentors, they only take requests after another agent has made an attempt at resolving the problem or during overflow situations.

2.1.4 Other Reasons to Add More Tiers

So far we have evaluated request volume, variability, and complexity and their roles in implementing additional tiers of support. There are other valid reasons to consider adding additional tiers of support. One of the most common reasons is the need to dispatch technicians to the desktop. If your service center has to provide hardware support, you certainly can't do that over the phone, and you certainly do not want tier 1 agents abandoning their stations to go to the customer's desk to swap out a pair of speakers or a mouse. Typically, groups that are going to be dispatched are established as a tier 2 resource pool. You can justify the additional overhead and complexities of having a second tier even though the requests may not be variable or complex. The justification is based on the need to provide dispatch support and the need to have tier 1 agents available to manage request volume. Often, hardware support is outsourced and structured as a tier 2 resource pool being tasked by tier 1. When the support is outsourced, you need to manage the outsourced function as a separate pool so that you can closely measure the usage and performance of the resources against any service level agreements (SLAs) you have in place.

If you do not have tools that allow your agents to take remote control of customer workstations, you will inevitably have to dispatch resources to the desktop to resolve problems. As with hardware support, any dispatched group is a good candidate for a tier 2 resource pool.

Beyond dispatch, there are still other valid reasons to implement additional tiers of support. A classic reason is security and control. Suppose your customers request changes to global mailing lists or group access rights. It would not be appropriate to provide all tier 1 agents with administrator rights to make those types of changes. Where requests require system administration (SA) rights, you should consider a multitiered model in which the requests are routed to the appropriate pool of system administrators.

Thus far we have discussed only two tiers of support. Very often, service centers have three or more. Use the same decision-making criteria you used to add the second tier when you consider additional tiers of support. Consider volume, variability (specialization required), complexity, outsourcing, security, and control. Typically, tier 3 resources include pools such as internal developers for products developed and/or maintained in-house and external help desks for the off-the-shelf products you support. They also include groups such as your metro and wide area network carriers, ISPs, and any other groups from which your company buys products and services. Tier 3 resources are usually not full-time service center employees; they generally have other responsibilities within the company, perhaps as internal developers or architects, or they might even work for outside companies, such as software vendors.

▶ 2.2 Managed Response Model

The managed response model is very similar, at least from an organizational perspective, to the immediate response model. There are three primary differences:

1. The customer uses alternative methods to contact the service center.
2. You have a chance to manage the assignment and completion of the requests to efficiently balance the workload.
3. You have the chance to prioritize the requests and handle them in an order other than first in/first out (FIFO), as in the immediate response model.

For example, if a request arrives via email during your peak load hour from 9:00 A.M. to 10:00 A.M., you have the opportunity to delay the response to that request until, say, 10:30, when your peak load is over and more resources are available. A managed response model is shown in Figure 2–4.

Notice that the organization of the resources that handle the request in the managed response model is no different than the structure of the immediate response model. The same people can handle these requests. Just as in the immediate model, how the calls are routed to the appropriate queue depends on your tool set. Many help desk systems now have the ability to automatically log, prioritize, and route the request to a queue. If you do not have these tools, these tasks must be done manually.

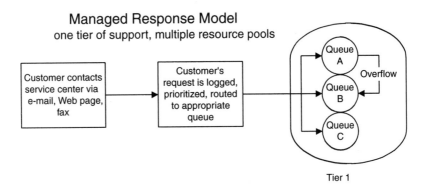

Figure 2–4   A managed response model with one tier of support.

The primary advantage to the managed response model is that it allows you to distribute workload and smooth out the peaks and dips in request volume. It also allows you to route requests to the most appropriate person or pool. This approach does have disadvantages, though. By definition, the managed response model delays the servicing of the request, which may not be acceptable to the customer. A more significant disadvantage is that it has the potential to actually generate more calls to the service center than if the request had been initiated over the phone in the first place. This occurs because the agent who handles the request will often have to contact the customer to gather additional information. If the customer is away from his or her desk, the agent must leave a message and either wait for a return call or make a follow-up call. It may take several calls before the agent and the customer actually connect, and return calls often come at inopportune times, when the agent has turned his or her attention to other tasks. It is also more difficult to gather resolution time metrics about the request, because work may be done when the agent is not on the phone with the customer, so typical call metrics are not available.

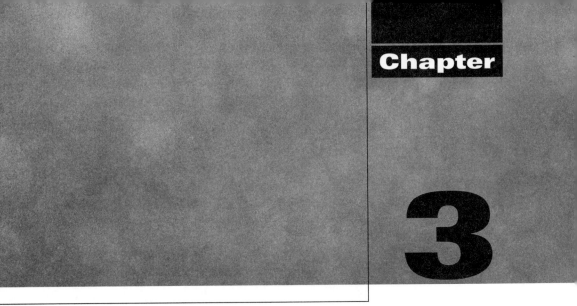

Maintaining a Service Catalog

A service catalog is a list of all the services you provide, and it has many implications for the service center. The service catalog will help you

- *Define services.* The catalog allows you to precisely describe the scope of each service, what is and is not included. You can also document the anticipated time it will take to perform the service (a service level).
- *Communicate the scope of services.* The service catalog is an excellent tool for clearly communicating the service centers' scope of work to management, customers, and service center employees.
- *Define Responsibility.* For each service in the catalog, you can define the service center's responsibility as well as the customer's.
- *Define the required resources.* Identifying the services you will provide allows you to define the areas and levels of expertise required of your service agents, which will make staffing your service center a more decisive process. Defining the anticipated volume of requests for each service will help you to determine the number of resources required.
- *Identify the support tools required.* Choosing the right hardware, software, communications equipment, and other tools (discussed further in Chapter 11, "Service Center Tools") is

essential to the productivity of your service center. Your list of services will help you select the tools that enable your staff and customers to work efficiently.

- *Develop a responsibility matrix.* A responsibility matrix defines who is responsible for delivering each service on your list. Requests for service are routed to the service agents or resource pools best suited to deliver groups of services that require related skills.

- *Define the structure of the organization.* You can define number of tiers required and the pools within each of tiers required to field those calls by identifying the skills required to support each service and the anticipated volume (see Chapter 2, "Service Center Organization" for further discussion). Many service centers create pools of resources with common skills to deliver subsets of the services you provide. This accommodates the incredible variety of products that most service centers support. Based on the complexity of the environment (products and services) you support, you can determine the tiers of support required to handle requests. In many service centers, the first tier of support handles the bulk of requests and therefore the most common requests. More complex problems are handled at a subsequent tier, tier 2. Tier 1 acts as a filter for all of the requests coming to the service center filtering out, in many cases, over 80 percent of the requests. Requests that take longer or require specialized skills, in-depth knowledge, or a dispatched agent are usually handled by tier 2. Those requests requiring even more skills or more time pass through to tier 3, and so on.

- *Determine Service Levels.* Determining the level of service you will provide for each service listed in your catalog will assist you in creating service level agreements (SLAs) and service contracts that (1) meet your customers' needs and (2) stay within the bounds of your center's capabilities.

- *Develop projected costs.* By determining the anticipated volume of requests for a service and the type of resources and amount of time required to provision the service, you can develop a service center budget.

- *Identify service metrics.* For each of the services in the catalog, identify the metrics you want to gather. You will see that many, if not most, of the metrics you identify will be the same across the services. However, you may also identify metrics that are unique to a particular service or group of services. For example, you may find that it is necessary to gather additional performance metrics for outsourced services in the catalog to ensure that your vendors are meeting their service commitments as documented in their service contracts.

Because the service catalog has such an important role within the service center, it should be formally maintained. Adding a new service can impact the structure of the organization and the skill sets required. A new service has to have service levels defined, escalation rules defined, and priority handling defined. There are costs associated with providing new services, and those costs must be evaluated. You may find that it is cheaper to outsource the service than to provide it internally.

Removing services from the catalog should be handled formally as well. They can be removed when they are no longer in use or when it is no longer cost effective to provide the service. In either case, removing services requires formal processing so as not to leave customers without support.

Formally maintaining the catalog means using structured processes to keep the catalog up-to-date and accurate, with these key objectives in mind.

1. Formally evaluate the services you provide.
2. Maintain the service catalog so that it always reflects current services.

The structured processes to maintain a catalog are Add a Service and Remove a Service, discussed in sections 3.1 and 3.2.

▶ 3.1 Add a New Service

Adding a new service to the service catalog is not as trivial a task as it may initially seem. While it is easy to add the service to the catalog, it is not necessarily so easy to deliver the service when a customer places the request.

A service center should implement a formal process that prepares all aspects of the service center to successfully deliver a new service. This includes all levels of the service center staff, service center management, and customers.

Many decisions must be made in advance to successfully implement the provision of a new service. In many ways, deploying a new service is similar to deploying new software, so a lifecycle approach should be taken. You must determine whether to outsource the service provision or train internal personnel. What are the costs of providing the service internally compared to outsourcing them? How many requests for the new service are anticipated, and how many people will be required to handle them? How will the new service be marketed to customers? Will customers require training in order to use the new service? How will we provide the service, and what steps are necessary to implement it? What timeframe must we work within? How do we measure our success?

The diagram in Figure 3–1 shows the tasks, at a high level, involved in adding a new service to the service center's offerings.

Generally, new service offerings will be identified from one of several sources.

- A new product may be purchased and deployed for the customer base, necessitating a new service offering.
- A new product may be developed and deployed for the customer base, necessitating a new service offering.
- Enough requests come from the customer base to justify the creation of a new service offering.

Purchasing new products and developing new products are not in the control of the service center and probably never will be. The key to successfully implementing a support service for these types of deployments is to be involved in the development and/or purchasing lifecycle process long before the product is deployed. This allows the service center time to prepare for implementing the service support of the product.

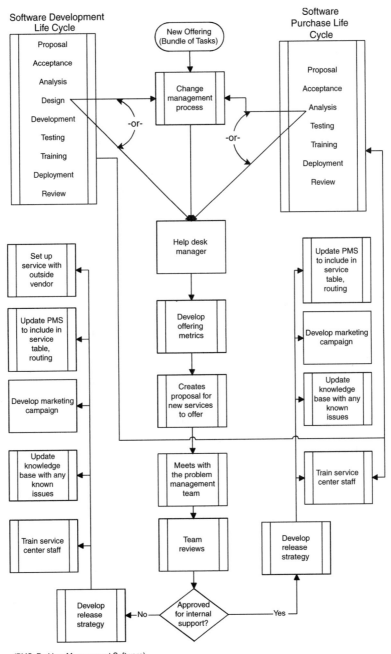

(PMS: Problem Management Software)

Figure 3–1 Add a new service to the service center's offerings.

The one source that is under the control of the service center is requests from customers. When enough requests come into the service center for a particular service, it may make sense for the service center to formalize the service and add it to the catalog. For example, suppose over the course of 6 months, there were three or four departmental moves, and the service center knew that more were coming. It would probably be worthwhile to create a new service specifically for group moves. This service is essentially a bundle of tasks and work orders, and most likely, processes are already in place for some of the tasks involved. Certainly, the service center already has a service for employee moves, which can serve as a basis for developing a group-move process. You would then create additional work order templates, logistics forms for the customers to fill out, project schedule templates, moving checklists for the service center and customer use, and other helpful tools, as necessary to cover the added tasks. While moving a department would be similar to moving an employee, it would also include tasks such as telecommunications consulting to design and implement a new phone system layout for the group. All of the tasks related to the group move would be predefined as part of the service offering. Some of the work could be handled by the service center and some by other groups, both internal and external to the company. The institutional knowledge of all aspects of moving a group would be documented as a service instead of just existing in someone's head. Imagine how professional this would be and how competent the service center would appear from the customers' perspective. Obviously, a service of this magnitude is not a short-term goal, but given time and discipline, it is completely possible.

3.1.1 Add a New Service Process

As mentioned above, the key to adding a new service is for the service center manager to be involved as early as possible in the product deployment lifecycle. For development projects, the optimal time is during the design phase, and for purchases, the optimal time is during the analysis phase.

Once the service center manager undertakes the effort to develop a new service offering, he or she must begin by developing metrics about the offering—primarily, cost estimating metrics, including all the standard cost and benefit data that would be gathered for any product or service.

- How many man-hours of effort will be required to provide an occurrence of the service?
- Is training required? If so, what will it cost?
- How many calls a day, week, or month are expected in the first 3 to 6 months, and beyond?
- What is the projected average internal cost per occurrence?
- How much would it cost to outsource the support for this particular service?

Based on this information, the service center manager would create a standard proposal to present to the problem management team. The problem management team would then review the proposal to determine if the support should be provided internally or outsourced. Notice that there is not a third option to not provide the service. When products are being deployed or calls are coming in for a service not already in the catalog, the service center has no choice but to provide the service. The key decision is whether to provide the support internally or externally, and then whether to formalize the recurring requests into a new offering.

If the decision is to handle the request internally, then the service center must create a release strategy (a plan). The plan should focus on a number of important items.

- Training the service center staff so that they have the skills necessary to provide the service.
- Updating the catalog to include the new service and its associated routing requirements, work order templates if applicable, and so on.
- Updating the knowledge base with any known issues, if applicable.
- A marketing campaign to inform and, if necessary, train the customer base.

If the service center management team decides to outsource the service, then a service contract must be established with an outside vendor. A marketing campaign will still be required, as will updates to the catalog and the knowledge base. The service center staff, however, will require only minimal training that focuses on the administrative handling of the new service.

Many different templates could and should be developed to support this process. Templates will standardize the process and essentially make it less difficult. There should be standard templates for:

- new service proposals
- cost/benefit metrics
- cost/benefit analysis
- service description (all the components to describe the offering)
- new service bulletin
- any other support information required by your company

▶ 3.2 Remove a Service

Removing a service from the catalog of supported services should be done proactively. That is, only services actively supported should be in the catalog to begin with. The Remove a Service process (shown in Figure 3–2) is initiated when

- The service center determines that a service they are providing is too expensive.
- The customer tells the service center that they will no longer need a supported product or service.
- A new IT standard eliminates a supported product or service.

If the effort is initiated by the service center, then the service center manager must develop a business case to support the removal. The case should focus on support costs, which must be unusually high (or why bother?), or else the product or service must be shown to negatively impact other parts of the infrastructure (e.g., the product may be the root cause of many other problems).

The business case must present alternative products or services and clearly indicate their benefits, such as lower support costs, better fit with standards, stability, features, less impact on other components, and so on. This part of the case will almost certainly involve other groups within IT, and perhaps the customer as well. In some instances the alternative may be as simple as upgrading to a newer version of a product. In other cases, it may mean that new software must be selected and data migrated from the old software to the new. The latter case is not a trivial task and would certainly require a compelling business case to justify both the capital outlay required and the inconvenience to the customer.

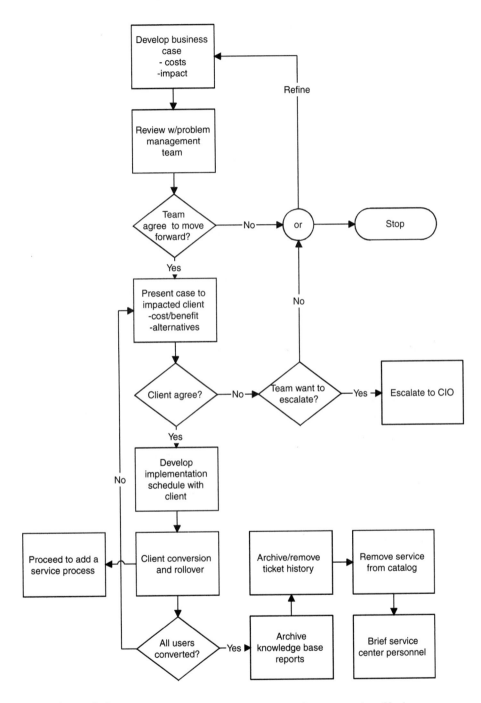

Figure 3-2 Remove a service from a service center's offerings.

Once the case is developed, the service center manager (SCM) presents it to the problem management team (PMT). If the PMT agrees with the business case (that the product or service should be removed), then the next step is to meet with the client(s). The PMT may also ask the SCM to refine the business case prior to meeting with the client. The business case must be solid before proceeding, because these undertakings are rarely an easy sell. Good metrics showing support costs of the current product or service compared with the proposed alternative will never embarrass the service center in management's eyes. Removal of a service is strictly a business decision based on cost and benefit analysis—there is nothing personal and no IT purist's zeal involved.

The case and the alternatives are presented to the client. If the client agrees, then a schedule must be developed for the deployment of the replacement product or service, if one is required. If the client does not agree, the PMT may drop the issue or escalate it to the CIO. There are many alternatives from there, including outsourcing the support and directly charging the support back to the customer. This is effective (especially if the support is expensive), but doesn't particularly foster good will.

Once the client has agreed to remove the product or service, and the replacement, if required, is deployed, then the service center can begin to clean up the service support system. First, the replacement product or service should be added using the Add a Service process. Then the associated knowledge base reports should be archived, and the tickets associated with the product or service should be archived or removed. The product or service should be removed from the service catalog. Finally, the service center team should be briefed so that future calls for the product or service can be caught in the validation process and handled like any other product or service that is not supported, perhaps by referring the request elsewhere.

Problem Identification

The first step in the problem management process is problem identification (see Figure 4–1). Problem identification is simply the processes, methods, and tools used by the service center to identify problems. Problems must be discovered and then reported to the service center. Problems, incidents, and requests are discovered by customers, IT staff, service center agents, and monitoring tools. The problems are then reported to the service center through a variety of access methods, including telephone, email, a Web gateway, tool-to-tool interfaces, person-to-person communication, and facsimile. Any or all of these access tools can be employed by a service center. Choosing the right combination of access tools and identification approaches to use depends on several factors, including the types of customers you support, the tools you have in place, the volume of problems and requests identified, the location of your customers, your service delivery goals, and your budget.

The key objectives in problem identification are to

1. Identify as many problems as possible proactively.
2. Make communication, or access, to the service center easy, fast, and consistent.

The best of all possibilities is to identify and eliminate problems before they impact your customers. A world-class service organization must be proactive in preventing or resolving customer problems before customers even know they have one. There are two ways to be proactive.

1. Identify situations before they become problems.
2. Identify and repair problems before the customer is impacted.

It is extremely important for the service center to keep track of the proactive work being done.

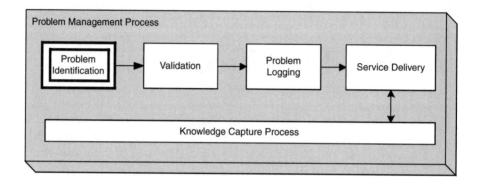

Figure 4–1   Problem identification is the first step in the problem management process.

▶ 4.1 Problem Discovery

Problems can be discovered either before they occur or after they occur. Discovering conditions that will eventually cause a problem—before the problem occurs—allows the service center to be proactive and to fix those conditions before a customer suffers any downtime. If you don't discover those conditions in advance—if you become aware of them only after they create a problem—then you are forced to fix the problem reactively. Many service centers, or help desks, today operate in a 100 percent reactive environment. This is a tough environment to work in because you are constantly putting out fires, which can be very stressful. If you are supporting external customers, there may not be much you can do to proactively eliminate problems in their environments. If you are supporting internal clients, there are many opportunities to be proactive and eliminate problems.

In a reactive service center, customers discover most of the problems. The customer is working, something bad or unexpected happens, and the customer reports it to the service center. The service center reacts by immediately setting out to isolate and fix the problem. Problems can also be discovered after the fact and reported by IT resources, the service center agents, and monitoring tools. Again, a problem occurs, it is discovered, and then it is reported through various access mechanisms.

In a service center with proactive capabilities, customers discover a smaller percentage of the problems, which is of course highly desirable, because the customer experiences fewer problems. Ideally, the service center either discovers the problem and fixes it before it affects the customer or identifies and fixes conditions that would have resulted in a problem for the customer. IT resources, product vendors, and monitoring tools discover problems or conditions that can lead to problems and report them to the service center. For example, IT resources, such as a testing team, may discover a problem with software released into the customer environment. The IT development group can then fix the problem and release a patch before any customers are affected. A vendor may publish a list of known bugs and workarounds, which the service center can distribute to customers before the customer has a problem. Monitoring tools have agents that monitor predetermined thresholds for important hardware and software deployed in the customer environment. When a component reaches the threshold, the monitoring tool alerts the service center, which can then proceed to fix the condition before a real problem occurs. The key to problem discovery is for the service center to identify problems or conditions that will cause problems before the customer is impacted. This allows the service center to reduce customer problems and downtime, and thereby reduce calls and the amount of immediate service that must be provided.

▶ 4.2 Problem Reporting Access

Independent of when a problem is discovered, before or after it impacts the customer, the service center must have methods and processes in place for the problem to be reported. Generally, problems can be reported using various tools and technologies.

The telephone is the most common method of access, particularly for problems reported by customers. Because the telephone has been used for so long as a service center access method, there are numerous add-on tools available that can improve and enhance the access for both the customer and the service center. Automated call distribution (ACD) systems, discussed in Chapter 12, "Service Center Tools," give the customer access to the person or persons best suited to deal with their problem. An interactive voice response (IVR) system can not only give the customer access to the service center, but can also offer a solution or acknowledge the problem so that the service center agents do not have to take the call. In many service centers, most, if not all, problems are reported using the phone as the access method. While this is an easy and convenient method, it does mean that the service center must be staffed up to receive the reports and provide immediate support to the person reporting the problem. To reduce the amount of immediate response support, many service centers are providing electronic access.

Electronic access hasn't been around as long as the telephone access, but equally robust tools are available to give customers and IT personnel simple, fast, and efficient access to the service center. Customers and IT alike can report problems via email or by using a Web-based form. Both are simple and allow users to describe the problem at their leisure, without having to wait on the phone in a telephone queue. This also allows the user to cut and paste information and screen shots so that they have less work to do to report the problem. Electronic access reduces the volume of calls and thus reduces the number of immediate response resources required.

Person-to-person reporting is used significantly less often as a problem reporting method than either the phone or electronic access, but it is still used by most service centers. One person discovers a problem and reports it to another, who can likely resolve it. Person-to-person is less popular because it requires that the people involved be at the same location. Further, like the telephone, the person reporting the problem expects immediate access. Unlike the telephone, there is generally no automatic routing to get the person and his or her problem to the person best suited to handle it.

Tool-to-tool communication is now a fairly common access method for reporting problems. The types of tools and access we are discussing here involves desktop and network management tools that discover problems or conditions that will lead to problems, and then automatically report the incidents through an interface to the service center's problem management system (PMS). People are not involved in either the discovery or the reporting. This is an extremely efficient way to streamline the entire problem identification process, while providing problem discovery and reporting on a 24/7 basis. See the Chapter 11 for a more thorough discussion.

4.2.1 Single Point of Contact

One of the most important things you can do to improve problem reporting is provide a single point of contact for all problems. While there may be different access methods, as discussed above, all infrastructure problems should be reported to a single entity, the service center.

A typical problem identification model for an internal service center is shown in Figure 4–2. The model shows both problem discovery and reporting. The dashed lines indicate that not all problems are reported. One of the first things to notice in the diagram is all the different places that customers in this model can go, or may have to go, to report a problem or request. In this model, the customer contacts the software development group when he or she has a problem with an in-house developed or maintained application, such as the purchasing system. If the customer has a telecommunication problem or request, he or she contacts the telecommunications group. For traditional desktop software or networking problems, the customer contacts the service center, a passing technician, or another customer. So what's the big deal? There are several big problems with this reporting diversity. First and foremost is that it is not easy for the customer to know what to do with the request or problem. Who should he or she contact? Further, a reported problem may span multiple technology groups. Is it a problem with a corporate application or with the network? Another big problem is that each of the groups that are outside of the service center, such as development and telecom in this model, must implement the same capabilities as the service center. They may not implement a full-blown service center, but they must have similar capabilities to identify, receive, and process customer problems and requests. If they are done informally, they are probably not done well. Customers can become so frustrated in this model that they just give up and don't bother reporting problems. Finally, there is no centralized IT view of the customers' experience, while the customer has a very clear view of IT.

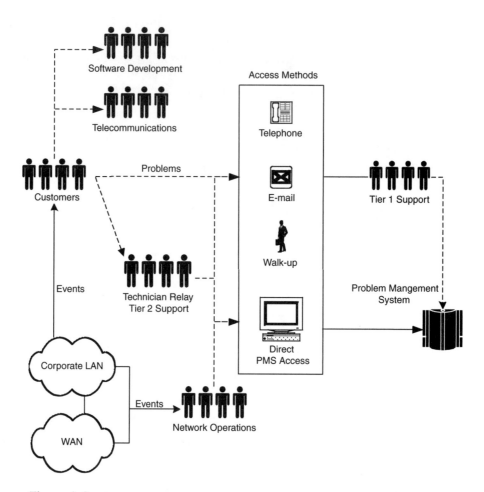

Figure 4–2 Problem identification model for an internal service
center.

If your service center operates using this model or some similar variation, one of the first things you should consider doing is creating a single point of contact for all problems and requests. You are
implementing a service center or help desk to formally handle problems
and requests, so it is not a stretch to extend that capability for additional problems and requests. You may not be able to do it all at once,
and in fact it may not be desirable. Consider getting your service center
up and running smoothly, and then incrementally adding support for
those rogue groups. If your service center is not favorably reviewed,
don't consider trying to convince the customers or management that
you would be best suited to handle all problem identification.

Chapter **4** I Problem Identification

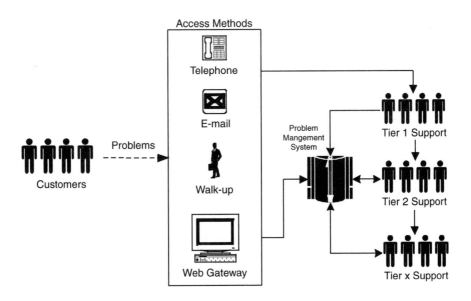

Figure 4–3   Typical external problem identification.

Single point of contact benefits the company by

- Making life easier for customers.
- Consistently applying problem management processes to all customer problems and requests.
- Eliminating redundant capabilities.
- Gathering better metrics on everything that is happening in the environment. Better metrics mean better control, which leads to more efficient service and all around IT performance.

If you support external customers only, your environment is probably a little cleaner and may be similar to the model in Figure 4–3.

In the model shown in Figure 4–3, customers experience a problem or have a request, and contact the service center using one of the available access methods. In many service centers, the four primary ways for a customer to access the service center is via telephone, email, walk-up, or Web-gateway. There are two big concerns with this setup. First, not everything that is identified is reported, and the model lends itself to being nearly completely reactive, unless you own and/or operate the infrastructure that serves the customer. A typical shrink-wrap software company that sells software to hundreds, thousands, or more customers has no control over the environment where their software is used and therefore cannot fix environmental problems before they occur. A local natural gas distribution company or cable company can be proactive, even though they are serving external customers, because they own and/or operate the infrastructure that serves the customer. While the infrastructure and monitoring tools may be different, these companies certainly reap the same benefits of being proactive in eliminating customer problems.

Many companies operate two or more help desks. One help desk will focus internally on supporting company employees (internal customers), while one or more help desks focus externally to provide service to external customers. Many companies do this because completely different skill sets are required at each help desk. Chances are that you support far more products and services internally than externally. Even if you are supporting an equally broad range of products internally and externally, it is nearly universal that they are different products and services, and therefore require different skill sets. Another good reason to separate the internal and external service centers and help desks is that the problem management processes used for external customers may be different than those used for internal customers. For example, external customers may purchase service and service contracts, while internal customers do not. Further, the subject trees and metrics gathered in support of external customers may be dramatically different than for internal customers.

▶ 4.3 The Proactive Service Center

The goal of a proactive service center is to eliminate customer problems before they generate a call for service. A single point-of-contact model, shown in Figure 4–4, is still desirable.

The two primary differences between this model and those shown in Figures 4–2 and 4–3 are the single point of contact and the infrastructure monitoring tools. The single point of contact means that the software development group and the telecommunications group now receive problem reports and requests through the service center. This enables two-way communication between the service center and the groups that are not part of the dedicated service center staff. Reports of defects and other problems or support requests from customers can be taken at the service center. You may or may not attempt to resolve them at the service center, but they are identified and consistently documented. If the development team identifies a problem, they can notify the service center while they are proactively fixing it. If the service center's PMS is interfaced with development's defect tracking system, the data need only be entered once. The same is true for telecommunications—problems and requests are identified and presented to the service center.

Figure 4–4 also shows infrastructure monitoring. Again, this is only applicable if you have some control over the infrastructure. If you do, the addition of monitoring tools allows you to proactively resolve problems before they occur or before the customers are affected.

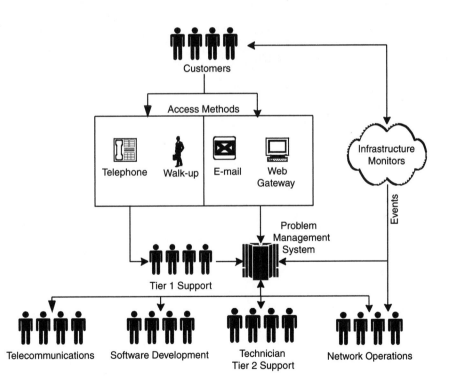

Figure 4–4 Single point-of-contact model for problem identification.

▶ 4.4 Implementation Considerations

If you do not currently identify problems proactively, you should initiate a project to identify and implement monitoring tools and agents across the entire infrastructure. The project should focus on developing a consistent, comprehensive, and affordable monitoring strategy. A representative from each of the disciplines (messaging, Internet, WAN, LAN, desktop, etc.) should participate in the evaluation, selection, and implementation of the tools and agents in their area. The service center must also be represented on the team, since they will be using the tools. A strong program/project manager must resolve issues, ensure overall compatibility, and own the overall implementation schedule. The project can be organized in a number of different ways, with a number of different participants, but there are several key factors:

- The strategy should be consistent and cross all of the disciplines, and all participants must work toward the same goals.
- This project requires strong leadership, negotiation, and team-building skills.

Integrate the monitoring tools and agents with the service center software. This can be done only after the tools and agents have been implemented and tuned. It can be done incrementally as each tool and agent has had a chance to mature in your environment.

For each type of significant event monitored, you must define the information that could be used to automatically populate a ticket; that is, for example, the category of the event, the priority level of the event, the routing of the ticket, the automatic notifications, and escalations.

You should evaluate the feasibility of integrating your private branch exchange (PBX) with your problem management system. This allows the PMS to pre-populate a ticket when a customer calls. When a record is automatically created, productivity increases and customers don't slip through the cracks.

Customer Validation

Customer validation is an important part of the problem management process and is illustrated in Figure 5-1. The primary goals of validation are to

1. Verify that the customer is a valid customer.

2. Deliver support only to valid customers.

3. Verify that the service requested is a valid service.

4. Verify that valid customers are eligible for the requested service.

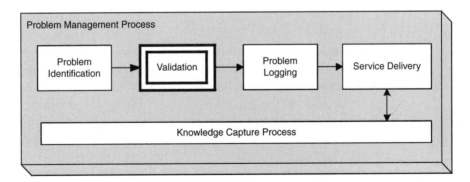

Figure 5-1   Validation is an important part of the problem management process.

45

5. Provide referrals and a value-added follow-up for referrals of legitimate contacts.

6. Track the number of requests from non-valid customers, requests for services not provided, ineligible requests, and the number of referrals.

Validating the customer means making sure that the person contacting the service center has the right to obtain services. For example, people from outside the company could call or email the service center (usually in error) and may not be eligible for services. It is important that the service center not give them information or access that could compromise security.

Validating the service simply means screening the contact to find out if the service requested is a service that the service center provides. If it is not, the legitimate contacts may be referred elsewhere. For example, suppose a customer calls the service center to buy one of your company's products, but the service center does not handle sales. The agent should refer the customer to the sales department. The referral can extend to include follow-up with the customer, which is a nice value-added service.

Finally, verifying eligibility means making sure that the validated customer is eligible to receive the service he or she is requesting.

The order in which to provide the validation will vary by service center. In some service centers, particularly those that service external customers, it may be beneficial to validate the requested service before taking the time to validate the customer. Suppose, for example, that you receive a lot of calls, in error, to support other companies' products. In this case, it would be best to validate that the service being requested is a service you provide before you take the time to validate that the customer is a valid customer. On the other hand, asking the customer which service they are requesting prior to validating that they are a valid customer can lead to a lot of wasted time. Suppose, for example, that you only provide free support to registered users for 90 days. A customer may call in and spend 5 minutes telling the agent about the problem before the agent has a chance to verify that the customer is registered and is within the 90-day limit. Determining the best approach depends on your particular circumstances. An automated call distribution (ACD) system (see Chapter 11, "Service Center Tools") can automate some of the screening for services supported and can be used to validate customers via a PIN, contract, or telephone number. The ACD, in conjunction with computer telephony integration (CTI), can successfully screen some, but not all, of the "bad" calls.

▶ 5.1 Typical Validation

In many service centers, particularly centers providing internal support only, the validation process is extremely informal. All three components of validation are usually considered, but are handled using a trust-based or casual policy approach. This occurs because the service center's culture is to provide service and help the customer in any way possible. Turning a customer down by not providing support can tarnish a service center's reputation. This typically happens to service centers that have a bad reputation to begin with. Usually, a close inspection of service centers in this situation reveals that too many aspects of the service center are run informally. There is a loose definition of the services that the center provides, no service level agreements (SLAs) with customers or suppliers, no performance measurement plan, and a serious lack of policies and other documentation. A loose, or informal, validation process can lead to further tarnishing of the service center's reputation. Suppose, for example, that a person calls the service center to request a new password. An informal validation process may give the caller access that he or she is not supposed to have. Many service centers have been scammed because they are victims of a poor validation process. A typical, informal validation process is shown in Figure 5–2.

When a request comes into the service center, the tier 1 staff looks for the user in a database. If the user is not found, then the service center opens a ticket under a manager's name and puts the contact's (new customer) name and other contact information in the Problem Description area of the ticket. A second ticket is created to add the new contact to the database. Often, an email is required from the manager before the new customer is added to the database of legitimate customers. While this approach is better than nothing, email is susceptible to forgery.

Whether the contact is a new user or not, the service center personnel next check to see if the request is a service provided by the service center. If it is not, the contact is given referral information, if it is known, and then the service center disconnects. A ticket is not started, and therefore there is no information on the volume of these requests or the amount of time spent on them.

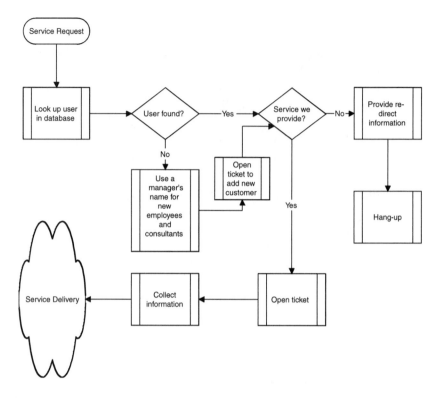

Figure 5–2 An informal validation process.

If it is a valid service, then a ticket is opened, the service center staff collect all the information, and the service delivery process starts. Many service centers consider all corporate employees (identified by calling on an "internal" line or by an employee ID number) and all corporate contractors as legitimate customers.

There are many problems and risks using this approach. Even if the request doesn't result in a security breach or some other malicious act, the service center may waste time providing support to non-customers when they could be supporting valid customers. Further, there are no metrics in this example on how often the problem occurs, at least for referrals. Such information is extremely valuable. The service center may get numerous calls for a service that isn't currently provided; if those calls were tracked, they could justify providing that service in the future. For example, suppose you do not currently support palm computing devices. Metrics showing continued increases in calls for that

Chapter **5** I Customer Validation

type of support would help justify the need to provide it in the future. Suppose you do not currently provide telecommunication support because the telecom group handles it and has their own support number, which customers are supposed to call. However, confused customers call you constantly and you must tell them the correct number to call. With good metrics, you could easily see the need to work with the telecom group. Your service center could then take the calls, gather the required information, and then forward the ticket to telecom, just as it does for any other tier 2 support group. The customer is better served because he or she only has to make one call.

If you are still in doubt about the need for formalizing validation, consider explaining to your management, after the fact, why your service center gave someone access to information they weren't supposed to see. In management's eyes, you will have no legitimate excuse.

▶ 5.2 Formal Validation

A formal validation process (shown in Figure 5–3) must be much more rigorous than the informal process. First, every contact with the service center should result in the generation of a service request ticket. This is critical for gathering metrics and managing the service center. These metrics can be used to support the addition of new services or may help establish a formal agreement for handling referrals. They could also lead you to an advertising campaign to educate your customers on what support you do provide.

An additional benefit of formalizing validation is that it allows you to move services to tier 1, or within tier 1. Suppose one of your goals is to close more calls at the initial point of contact, at tier 1. One way to accomplish that is to move services that have been traditionally resolved at tier 2 to tier 1. As an example, many service centers do not allow tier 1 agents to add or move customers to a new domain. Why? It is a simple task to perform and with minimal training could be done by a tier 1 agent. The reason, typically, is that validation at tier 1 is weak, so it falls upon the tier 2 agent to validate that the customer is allowed to have access to the services in the requested domain. A formal validation process at tier 1 would remove the concern and would allow you to handle a simple service at the initial point of contact. If you want to move simple tasks being done at tier 2 or 3 to tier 1, it is extremely important that more rigorous validation be implemented to ensure that only valid customers are receiving such services. Look to see if you have simple tasks being done at tier 2, 3, or beyond that could be done at tier 1 if formal validation were in place.

Any corporate policies regarding service eligibility, access, security, and so on should be enforced at this control point in the problem management process. For example, if a valid corporate user (who has a corporate login) calls in for support on a personal home computer (not purchased by the company), corporate policy may dictate that he or she is not eligible for service. This would be caught by the service center during the validation process and explained to the customer. The ticket would be closed at this point, before moving on to the Logging and Service Delivery processes.

If you plan to charge your customers on a per-incident basis or under a service plan, then validation is absolutely necessary. You must make sure the charges go to the right group or you may end up eating the costs. The customer paying the bill will certainly validate that they deserve the charges, so you must validate as well.

As the number of Internet and intranet service requests increases, formal validation will become a necessity. You must have some method of confirming that you should take the time and effort to provide the requested service to the customer.

▶ 5.3 Validation Process Description

All service requests received in the service center must result in the creation of a service request ticket (or simply, ticket). Some of those may be created automatically. Tickets created automatically will come from monitoring tools, email, Internet forms, and CTI. Tickets created manually will come from fax, walk-ups, and the telephone (a complete description of the sources of requests is provided in Chapter 4, "Problem Identification"). All tickets must be validated except those generated by the monitoring tools.

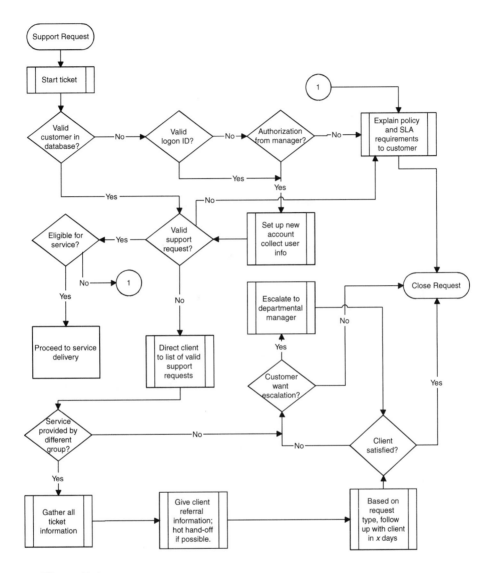

Figure 5–3 A formal validation process.

After creating the ticket, the service center agent must check to see if the requestor is a valid customer and listed in a database. If the requestor is a valid customer, then the agent checks to see if the request is for a valid service (one offered by the service center). If the person is not a valid customer in the database, for example, a new employee or contractor or a new external customer, the agent must check to see if the requestor has a customer ID. A valid customer ID could be a PIN number, a login ID, a product serial number, a service contract number, and so on. If the requestor has customer ID, then the agent should set him or her up as a valid customer, and then verify that the request is for a valid service.

If the requestor is not a valid customer in the database and they do not have some type of customer ID, then company policy should dictate how to handle the new customer. For an internal service center, many companies require an authorization from the manager. The policy should also indicate how the authorization is communicated. In this case, the agent must check to see if the customer or the service center has a valid authorization from a manager. Based on company policy, a valid authorization from a manager could be a standard email. A phone call could work but would not leave an audit trail, which is important for the service center to maintain.

If the requestor is not a valid customer and does not have a valid customer ID, but has an authorization from an appropriate manager, then the agent should set up the requestor as a valid customer in the database. The agent then checks to see if the new customer is requesting a valid service.

If the requestor is not a valid customer, does not have a customer ID, and the service center does not have an authorization from an appropriate manager, then the agent should explain the company policy to the requestor, direct him or her to the appropriate corporate manager, and then close the ticket. The agent should send a copy of the policy and the required authorization form to the customer or point him or her to the information on the service center's Web page. As with any request, the requestor could ask to have the issue escalated to the service center manager, in which case the ticket would be updated but not closed.

At this point, assume the customer has been validated. If the customer is requesting a valid service, then the agent must check to see if the customer is eligible to receive the requested service. Any corporate policies regarding service eligibility are enforced at this control point in the process. For example, if a valid corporate customer calls in for support on his or her personal home computer (not purchased by the company), corporate policy may dictate that they are not eligible for service. Other corporate policies, such as access control, should be enforced at this point in the process as well. In addition to policies, SLAs and service plans and contracts may contain information about eligibility. If you have these contracts in place and they specify eligibility for services, then the agent must have easy access to them and must refer to them at this point in the validation process. This is certainly more easily said than done. You don't want agents wasting vast amounts of time combing through policies, SLAs, contracts, plans, and other documentation. The best way to handle it is to show the agent the subset of services available under the customer's plan, SLA, or contract, and then when the agent selects the service requested by the customer, any eligibility rules for that service should be shown to the agent. If the requested service isn't governed under a contract, then the service selected should show the agent any eligibility rules, dictated by policy, that apply to that service. If your problem management system (PMS) does not have this capability, then a lot of training and other custom development may be required.

Again, based on company policy or contract, a valid customer may be eligible for some services but not others. If they are not eligible for the service requested, the agent should explain the policy or contract. The agent should then direct the requestor to the appropriate corporate manager and then close the ticket. As with any request, the requestor can ask to have the issue escalated to the service center manager, in which case the ticket would be updated but not closed.

If the requestor is a valid customer, is requesting a valid service, and is eligible to receive the requested service, then the agent proceeds to the service delivery process.

If the requestor is a valid customer but is requesting a service not provided by the service center, then the agent should direct the customer to a list of valid services. This could be an online catalog or a service center brochure. If the requested service is handled by a different group (internal or external), the requestor should be referred to that group. The service center should have agreements in place with any group to which they will be referring customers. When this is the case, the agent updates the ticket and marks it as a referral. The ticket can be kept open and a follow-up call given to the customer after a specified amount of time, based on the type of referral. This is a true value-added service. If enough calls are referred to a particular group, it may prove valuable for that group to have a copy of the problem management system and to act essentially as a tier 2 group for that type of service request.

▶ 5.4 Validation Implementation

To implement a formal validation process, you must develop a service catalog that clearly defines services, and you must develop policies in support of the validation requirements for each service. You must also develop and maintain a customer database that has some mechanism for validating customers. If you have contracts in place that contain eligibility rules, you need a mechanism that provides that information to the agents when they need it.

A clear, concise, and agreed-upon policy needs to be developed to define who a valid customer is and their authorization to obtain services from the help desk. The policy should address contractors and consultants, temporaries, new employees, and existing employees. It should define the documentation required for someone who is not in the database as a valid customer to obtain services (at minimum, require an email from a manager). It should also define default parameters for new customers based on customer type (contractors, temporaries, and so on).

Continually develop and modify policies regarding eligibility for services. If informal rules exist, formalize them and provide training to make sure everyone understands the new rules. If a customer is not eligible for a service, it is very nice to have a policy to fall back on as the good reason and it certainly portrays a higher level of professionalism.

A modified approach to the validation process is shown in Figure 5–4. The process assumes that all customers are on a service plan and that a plan sales department exists. The model is nearly identical to the formal validation process shown in Figure 5–3 in that each customer is validated, the service requested is validated, and the customer's eligibility for the requested service is validated. When the customer contacts the service center, it is assumed that the customer will provide a contract number. That contract number will be checked to see if the contract is valid. The contract essentially is a collection of applicable services (a service plan) and can be a standard plan or a custom plan. In either case, a service center agent or an automated system checks to see if the plan can be located. If it is not found, the customer is routed to the sales department in the case of a phone call, or to a Web page in the case of electronic service requests. If no sale is made, the ticket is closed. If a sale is made, the customer is routed to the appropriate group, usually based on the service level purchased in the plan.

In the case where the customer submits a request, the contract ID is validated (the plan is found). The agent must then validate that the customer is a valid customer according to the contract. Many service contracts specify the customers who are allowed to request services. If the contract is valid but the customer is not valid according to the terms of the contract, then the agent must explain the terms to the customer. After explaining the terms of the contract, the agent may send the customer on to sales so that the customer can be added to the contract, can purchase a new one, or can choose to close the ticket.

If the agent determines that it is a valid contract and a valid customer under the terms of the contract, then the agent must verify that the service requested is a valid service under the given contract or service plan. If it isn't, the agent explains the terms of the contract and then, at the customer's discretion, either routes the customer to sales or closes the ticket.

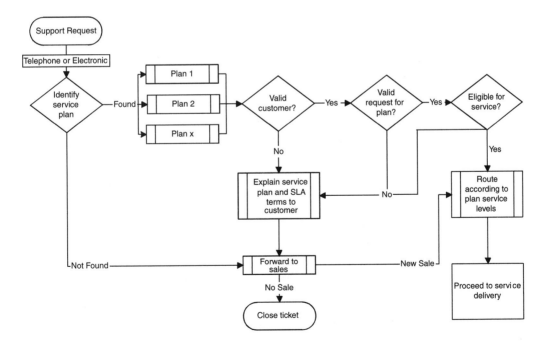

Figure 5–4 Service plan validation process.

If the agent determines that there is a valid contract, a valid customer, and a valid request, then the agent may need to verify eligibility. To a large extent, the need for this step will depend on the type of contracts in place. The contracts may be set up such that all customers named in the contract are eligible for all services in the contract, in which case, there is no need to verify eligibility once the contract, customer, and service have been validated. If this is not the case, then eligibility verification may be required.

The service delivery process starts after the contract, customer, requested service, and eligibility have been validated. Depending on the type of services and plans your service provides, some combination of the formal validation plan above and the service plan validation in Figure 5–4 may be required.

Problem Logging

The problem logging process is initiated after a service request has been identified and validated (see Figure 6–1). The purpose of the logging process is to create a centralized record of the service request (a ticket) and then categorize and prioritize the record for processing. There are three main components to problem logging. First, the service center agent must gather information. Next, when the agent has gathered enough information, he or she categorizes and prioritizes the problem. This often requires negotiation with the client. Finally, the agent documents the request (logs it) in a central location.

Problems can be detected and reported by customers, and they can be detected and logged automatically if infrastructure-monitoring tools are in use and interfaced with the problem management tool. Problems are documented in such a way that they can be handled and tracked until they are resolved. The key goals of problem logging are to

1. Provide a single point of contact for all customer problems and requests.
2. Document all problems in the same central location, the problem management system.
3. Accurately record all of the required information to track the problem from start to resolution.

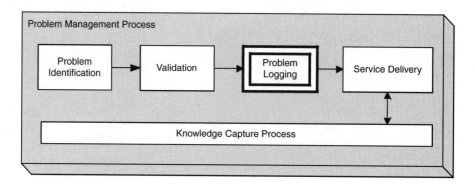

Problem Management Process

| Problem Identification | → | Validation | → | Problem Logging | → | Service Delivery |

Knowledge Capture Process

Figure 6–1   The problem logging process begins after identification and validation.

4. Rapidly collect the information required to categorize and resolve the request.

5. Accurately categorize the request for escalation, if required.

6. Accurately categorize the request for routing, if required.

7. Accurately categorize the request in order to improve knowledge base retrieval.

▶ 6.1 Current Problem Logging Approaches

In many service centers, problems are logged in multiple problem management systems (PMSs). For example, the telecommunications department may use a voice mail form and mailbox, the network operations team may use an extension of their monitoring tools, the mainframe operations team and mainframe application developers may have their own PMS, and the help desk, or service center, may have its own problem management tool. This setup usually occurs as a result of evolution. Each group has its own charter, areas of responsibility, and areas of expertise (mainframe applications versus desktop applications). Providing support in each of these independent areas grows as the customer use of the area grows. Each group has to provide support for its area, and so they all grow independently. Typically, this means that there are multiple help desks but no single service center.

So what? Why is this a problem? There are several problems with this approach. First, this means that there is no single point of contact, so a customer must know who to call for each request. Second, when one of the help desks receives a call, the problem they are trying to resolve will often overlap with another help desks area of responsibility, thus requiring coordination and sometimes leading to finger pointing between help desks. Each help desk most likely has its own problem management processes, all different, making it difficult for the customer to have reasonable expectations. Prioritization, escalation, and resolution times most likely vary from help desk to help desk. All of this makes it difficult for the customer to know what to expect. From the customer's perspective, IT looks somewhat ridiculous.

Another problem is that help desk resources cannot be used efficiently when they are completely segregated, as in this model. For example, the mainframe team may be having a slow day, while the networking team can't keep up with their calls. Further, problems that span multiple disciplines are more difficult to resolve when each group places a different priority on the problem and has different processes. Problem ownership becomes very difficult in this scenario.

From the IT management perspective, it is very difficult to create summarized information (metrics) across multiple help desks, because each group defines requests, priorities, and categories differently. Even if it can be done, it requires additional work.

Centralized problem logging eliminates many of these problems. First, understand that centralized logging is just the process used to implement a service center strategy. Usually, that strategy is to provide the customer base with a single point of contact for all service requests and problems. An additional benefit of this strategy is that it provides easy access to metrics that are used to span multiple help desks and multiple systems. Also, it usually means that one set of problem management processes, priorities, and categories will be implemented across all of the former help desk disciplines. The customer gains the ease of a single point of contact, which means that he or she need understand only one set of processes and priorities. Although it may require some coaching and encouragement, the diverse disciplines usually end up improving their working relationships, because in the end, they want to provide good service to their customers.

▶ 6.2 Future Problem Logging Methods

To reach this point in the problem management process, the service request has been initiated or the problem has been discovered and then validated (see Figure 6–1). During the validation process, a record of the contact was created if a customer originated the request. Internal IT and monitoring tools do not require validation or a separate contact record. The problem logging process begins by creating a ticket. If the service request originated from a monitoring tool, then the interface between the monitoring tool and the PMS should create the ticket and then give it the required category and priority and other necessary information. In other words, the interface should handle all of the problem logging steps automatically. If the service request originated from someone in IT, the originator should handle all of the problem logging steps, that is, creating the ticket and then categorizing, prioritizing, and documenting the request. This should be accomplished by giving IT resources direct access to the PMS.

If the service request originated from a customer, the service center personnel (an agent) must either categorize the request or review the category assigned by the customer. The customer may have provided a category, if he or she submitted an electronic service request (ESR). Even if the customer provided a category, an agent must review it for accuracy. If the customer submitted an ESR without a category, the tier 1 service center agent must review the correspondence to see if there is enough information to categorize and begin processing the request. If there is not enough information, the service center must contact the customer. The follow-up contact to the customer's ESR can be electronic or it can be a telephone call. If the customer called the service center or walked up to the service center, then the agent must have a conversation with the customer and execute the logging process.

If the agent is speaking with the customer, he or she asks the customer to explain the problem, asks specific questions as necessary, and then documents the customer request. Then the agent works with the customer to establish the priority of the ticket. The priority table and its description are given below. Next, the agent reads the documentation of the request, including the priority assigned, back to the customer and asks the customer if he or she agrees with the documentation. If the customer does not agree, then the discussion continues until the agent and customer reach agreement. At this point, the agent should have enough information to categorize the request. If not, then the agent continues asking questions and updating the documentation until enough information is gathered to categorize the request. Sample categories are shown in Figure 6–2.

Now the service request has resulted in a ticket, the issue has been documented to the satisfaction of the service center agent and the customer, and the ticket has been categorized. Remember the assumption that if the source of the ticket was a monitoring tool or an IT infrastructure request, the ticket already contains the required documentation and is categorized and prioritized. The final step in this process is to log the ticket.

The information required for problem logging varies, depending on its source. Table 6–1 shows the typical data that is required when a problem is logged. Nearly identical data is required for problems logged by service center agents and for problems logged via interfaces from monitoring tools. The primary difference is that the interface between the monitoring tool and the PMS should provide most of the information automatically.

6.2.1 Tier 1 Ticket Information

Traditionally, help desks handled problems only, not requests for service. This is changing for good reason. First of all, it makes life easier for customers when there is a single point of contact. Second, the help desk already has the tools to do the job. The contact methods are in place, agents are in place to take the call, a Web gateway and/or email is in place to take electronic requests, and processes are in place to ensure that contact from the customer doesn't "fall through the cracks" and that response is made in a timely fashion. A service request, like a problem report, requires that someone document the information, make a time commitment, route the information to the appropriate resource, escalate when necessary, and close the request when the service is delivered. So it is not a stretch to imagine that the traditional help desk could be extended to become a full-service center by adding additional services to their traditional problem-solving services.

Table 6–1 Data Required for Problem Logging

Ticket Information	Ticket Number
	Status
	Priority
	Incident Category (i.e., Printer)
	Incident Type (i.e., Printer)
	Incident Item (i.e., HPxxxx)
	Date/Time Opened
	Date/Time closed
	Opened by
	Closed by
	Current Owner
	Routing/Escalation History
Incident	Summary
	Detailed Description
	Instructions to Reproduce
	Related Incidents
Customer Information	Name
	Department
	Location
	Phone
	email
Customer Asset Information	Hardware Information
	Software Information
	Sub-net Information
	Telecom Information
Customer Open Incidents	
Customer SLA	
Resolution	Attempted Solutions/Workarounds
	Related Knowledge Base Report
	Additional Comments

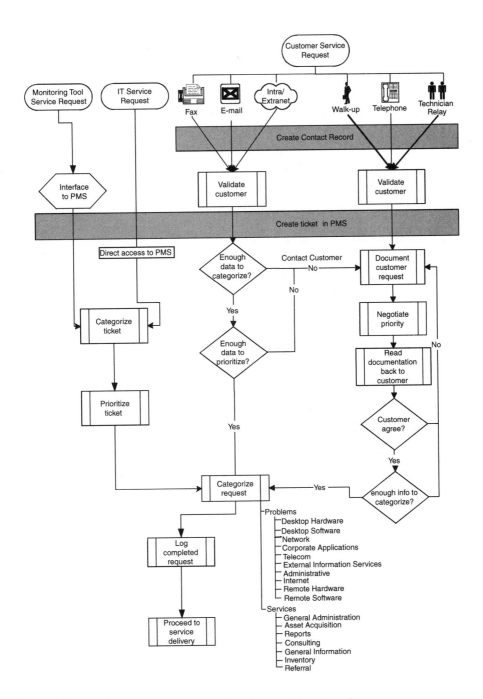

Figure 6–2   Sample categories for problem logging.

Traditional PMSs have evolved to handle the addition of services. Because of the similarities in handling between a request and a problem report, the evolved systems are not radically different. The underlying concept of a ticket as a record for each request is used for both requests and problems. Workflow for routing and approvals is used for both. A subject tree approach is used for both. Finally, as with traditional PMSs, data collection forms can be customized based on the type of problem or request to ensure that agents gather the correct data.

The information collected for a service center ticket will vary according to the type of request. For example, a request for service, such as software training, requires different information than is required for a problem report, such as hardware failure. However, the ticket information for both has much in common. What is important is that you capture the information required to process the request, no matter what type, then centrally log the request and apply the necessary service delivery processes and controls to satisfy the customer. The basic information required for a problem is shown in Table 6–1.

▶ 6.3 Service Request Categories Overview

The service center handles many different types of service requests. All requests, whether for routine service or for problem resolution, are considered service requests. Many service centers document the service request categories in a subject tree. The way you choose to organize service requests is extremely important for several reasons.

- Routing and escalation workflow of a ticket is often based on categories.
- The attributes/fields of the ticket form may change based on the selected category.
- The ease with which an agent can find and select the correct category is based on the organization of the categories.
- Measurement data is based on the categories.

The automatic routing and/or escalation of a ticket in many PMSs is based on the type, or category, of the ticket. For example, if a tier 1 agent categorizes a ticket as a hardware problem, then the system can be set up to automatically route the ticket to the tier 2 resource pool that handles hardware problems. Automatic routing is important because it reduces training requirements and routing mistakes. It also allows you to change service responsibilities without retraining the entire staff. You can route to individuals or pools and can even identify second or third pools to route to when certain predefined conditions are true for the primary pool. In many ways, automatic routing in the PMS is similar to the routing provided by an automated call distribution (ACD) system.

Many PMSs will select a ticket form based on the category selected. Using a different form for different categories allows you to ensure that agents gather the data required for the category of the request without having to provide them with extensive training. For example, if the agent selects the category for an employee move, an employee move ticket is presented to the agent to make sure the agent gathers the data required to start a work order for the move. If the agent selects the category for a desktop software problem, a different form is used. As discussed previously, the forms will be different, but there will be overlap.

The categories are normally organized as a hierarchy, which is often referred to as the subject tree. The agent finds the right category by "drilling down" through the subject tree. For example, the agent may start by selecting that the request is a problem, then select that it is a desktop software problem, then select the correct desktop software package, and then select from a predefined list of common problems with that particular package. The agent needs to accomplish this drill-down quickly and efficiently, so it is very important that the hierarchy is organized both simply and intuitively. If the hierarchy is too complex, it may take additional time for the agent to find the correct category. That additional time can really add up over the course of a year. If the categories are not organized intuitively, the agent may not be able to find the category at all. An incorrectly categorized ticket is a big problem. The agent may not gather the correct information, the ticket may be incorrectly routed, and service center metrics will be incorrect.

Many important metrics are gathered based on the service center categories. You will undoubtedly rely on many of these measurements to manage the service center. Tracking volumes by category gives you information, for example, on how many problems you have had with a specific product, such as a particular brand of printer, or even one particular printer. This data can then be "rolled up" to the next higher level to show how many problems you have had with all printers. It can be further rolled up as part of the summary data on the total number of all hardware-related problems, which in turn can be rolled up as part of the information for all reported problems.

Don't forget that your plan lays out specific measurable objectives and the way this hierarchy is organized can help you measure the achievement of those objectives. Suppose, for example, that one of your objectives is to reduce the average number of calls per workstation by 3 percent by the end of the year. One of your strategies to accomplish this is to identify and replace troublesome hardware. Obviously, the ability to keep track of problems related to specific pieces of hardware or brands of hardware (or both) may well help you achieve that goal. There are other ways of gathering important data besides rolling it up the hierarchy, but it all starts by categorizing the tickets. For example, you may suspect that the hardware failure rate at a certain location in the building is higher than anywhere else in the building. Using a combination of the roll-up information and location attributes, you could run an ad hoc query to retrieve all of the tickets and statistics about hardware problems in that location.

How you choose to organize the categories depends on the automatic routing, notification, and alerting you choose to deploy, the variation of data required to handle requests, the ease and intuitiveness of use by the agents, and the metrics you want to gather. One important note: It is important that you keep track of work done proactively in support of the customer service base. You can either create a category in the hierarchy for proactive work or create an attribute on the ticket. Since the same work can be done proactively or reactively, it may be best to use an attribute on the ticket as opposed to a separate category in the hierarchy. This will prevent you from having two nearly identical lower level hierarchies.

For illustrative purposes in Figure 6–2, the categories are broken down at the highest levels into Problems and Services (value-added). Breaking the service requests into these two broad categories allows the service center to easily distinguish calls for problems from calls for services. If you were to use this approach, it would also be important for you to keep track of other information that wasn't captured by the hierarchy, for example, whether the work was done proactively versus reactively, which means keeping track of who initiated the request, among other facts.

The key goals in creating an effective list of service request categories are

1. Keep the category list as simple and intuitive as possible, so that the service center agents can easily and accurately categorize problems.
2. Make sure the list is comprehensive enough to cover the entire scope of services.
3. Create a list that is robust enough to allow for meaningful management metrics for each category.
4. Create a list of categories that maps easily to service center resource pools and maps to only one pool at each level.

6.3.1 Service Request Categories Hierarchy

Another sample service request category hierarchy, or subject tree, is shown in Figure 6–3. There are many possible variations, depending on the environment you support, on the automatic routing, notification, and alerting you want to deploy, the various data required to handle requests, the ease and intuitiveness of use by the agents, and the metrics you want to gather.

6.3.2 Service Request Category Definitions

As previously mentioned, the hierarchy can be organized in a nearly infinite number of ways. Therefore, descriptions of only a few of the categories are given below.

Problem

For our purposes, a problem, or an incident, occurs any time a customer, including IT customers, cannot complete some task they are trying to accomplish, using a computer and/or computer-related equipment, such as software or the network. Problems can be resolved proactively, and in that case, it is important to capture that information.

```
1.  Problem                                       2.1.2.    New Employee
    1.1.    Desktop Hardware (HW)                  2.1.3.    Exit Employee
        1.1.1.    Printer                      2.2.    Asset Acquisition
            1.1.1.1.    Hewlett-Packard 4SI     2.2.1.    Desktop HW
        1.1.2.    Monitor                          2.2.2.    Desktop SW
        1.1.3.    Mouse                            2.2.3.    Remote/Mobile
        1.1.4.    CPU                                  2.2.3.1.    Laptop
    1.2.    Desktop Software (SW)                        2.2.3.2.    Palm Device
        1.2.1.    Operating System                     2.2.3.3.    CE Device
            1.2.1.1.    NT                       2.2.4.    Pager
            1.2.1.2.    Office 98                2.2.5.    Cellular Phone
            1.2.1.3.    Linux                2.3.    Telecom
        1.2.2.    Microsoft Office                 2.3.1.    Upgrade Phone
            1.2.2.1.    Microsoft Word           2.3.2.    New Voice Mail Box
            1.2.2.2.    Microsoft Excel          2.3.3.    Expand Voice Mail Box
            1.2.2.3.    Microsoft Outlook        2.3.4.    Phone Card
            1.2.2.4.    Microsoft Access         2.3.5.    Set Up Video Conference
    1.3.    Remote HW                                2.3.6.    Feature Change
    1.4.    Remote SW                                2.3.7.    New Analog Line
    1.5.    Infrastructure                   2.4.    Reports
        1.5.1.    Hardware                         2.4.1.    Inventory
        1.5.2.    Software                         2.4.2.    Assets
    1.6.    Telecommunications                       2.4.3.    SLA
    1.7.    Corporate Applications           2.5.    Consulting
        1.7.1.    General Ledger                   2.5.1.    Desktop Application
        1.7.2.    Payroll                          2.5.2.    System Requirements
        1.7.3.    Risk Management                  2.5.3.    Personal Training
        1.7.4.    Human Resources                  2.5.4.    Special Support
    1.8.    Administrative                   2.6.    General Information
        1.8.1.    Password Reset                   2.6.1.    Phone Numbers
        1.8.2.    Change Login Script              2.6.2.    Policy
        1.8.3.    Modify Account Details           2.6.3.    Forms
    1.9.    Internet                         2.7.    Referral
    1.10.    External Information Services       2.7.1.    Training
        1.10.1.    Lexis - Nexis                        2.7.1.1.    Vendor 1
        1.10.2.    Reuters                              2.7.1.2.    Vendor 2
        1.10.3.    Bloomberg                        2.7.2.    Purchasing Department
2.  Value-Added Service                           2.7.3.    Accounting
    2.1.    General Administration
        2.1.1.    Move Employee
```

Figure 6–3   Sample service request category subject tree.

Value-Added Service

Value-added service requests come into the service center and result in one or more work orders or purchase orders being generated. Work orders can be thought of as projects. Some projects require change management processing, and some do not. The number of customers involved and impacted by the project can be used to make this determination. For hardware-specific projects, the use of the particular hardware can determine whether or not change management processing is required. For example, a change to a mission critical server would certainly require change management processing while a change to an individual's local printer would not. If set up properly, the service center can directly bill the customer for the services offered. Typical services that would result in the creation of work orders include employee moves, new employees, infrastructure upgrades and extensions, and so on.

Many PMSs can be extended to support the creation of work orders based on the type of project. Consider fully developing this section of service category table to identify what work has to be done, who will do the work, how long it should take, what approvals are required, and which services require change management approval.

Referral

To provide additional value-added services to the customer base, the service center should provide referral services. Referrals occur when a customer calls the service center to request a service that the service center, perhaps even the company, does not provide. Examples include training requests, which may be outsourced to various companies, depending on the type of training required. When a customer calls for training, the service center should open a ticket and refer the caller to the person in the company who schedules training, then close the ticket. Keeping a record of the contact provides you with important metrics. Other examples of services that may require referrals are requests for new furniture and requests to move boxes as part of an employee move. If you don't handle those tasks by generating and routing work orders, you should provide a referral service.

Asset Acquisition

These are usually assets purchased in support of the infrastructure. They can be hardware, software, or connectivity products that are not related to a particular customer, but instead are related simply to infrastructure, the company, or perhaps a department. It can be extended, though, to handle many common purchase requests, such as requests for desktop hardware and software, printers, mobile and remote equipment, cellular phones, and pagers.

Another important attribute to track regarding asset acquisition is, once again, proactive work. For example, you may order additional memory for a customer because your desktop management software reported that the customer's machine had sustained memory utilization above 80 percent. It is important to keep track of the number of problems you prevented because of proactive work done by the service center or by the rest of the IT team.

Feature Requests

Feature requests deal with a lack of functionality. A customer may call and specifically request new functionality for a product or may mistakenly report a problem to the service center that in reality is a feature request. This occurs when the customer believes that the product was designed to provide some feature that it was not designed to provide. You can gather the information and pass it on to the appropriate internal or external development team. At minimum, you want to keep a record of the call for your metrics.

6.3.3 Service Category Implementation

Work closely with your PMS vendor to identify the alternatives for implementing this list in the software. The category list has many different purposes. These include ticket routing, escalation, creation of an online service catalog, as well as consolidating metrics. The list also has different uses within the extensions to the problem management software, such as asset management, work orders, and purchasing. Work with the vendor to identify the best way to implement this list in the PMS.

If you're implementing a new PMS, take plenty of time to design your subject tree in advance, because the new service categories must be implemented for the system to work properly. It is very difficult to change your subject tree once it has been in use for a while. These categories are tightly coupled with the service catalog, which should also be completed prior to implementing the problem management system.

If you are migrating to a new system, map the categories used in the current PMS(s) to the subject tree designed for the new system. The mapping information will be required to migrate tickets from the current system to the new one.

You should also conduct the mapping if you are planning to centralize formerly decentralized service centers. This will help you create a comprehensive subject tree and will indicate where training is required. It will also help you to understand how tickets will be routed, and to organize appropriately.

Determine how much history to migrate from all existing PMSs into the new PMS. The amount will depend to a large extent on how much automation can be used to accomplish the task. A year's worth of tickets from the current system can be far too much to migrate if manual intervention is required.

▶ 6.4 Prioritizing Requests Overview

Clearly defined and well-understood problem priorities allow the service center to focus its resources so that the highest priority calls are handled first. Assigning priorities to calls, based on the impact of the reported problem, ensures that they are resolved in the most efficient manner. The priority will determine how quickly the service center will initially respond to a problem and will establish a target time for resolving the problem. The assigned priority is used to determine how the service center will deploy staff to address the problem and which staff to deploy. It will also determine an automatic notification and escalation schedule. Many service centers have a special team that responds immediately to all priority-one problems.

The priority also allows the agent to inform the customer of the response times, based on the selected priority level. It is important for both the service center staff and the customer to fully understand the definition of each priority.

When a call comes into the service center, the agent must negotiate and come to an agreement with the customer on the priority level of the problem. If the customer and the agent cannot reach agreement on the priority level to assign, the problem should be escalated to the shift manager or the service center manager.

Table 6–2   Service Center Priority Scheme and Definition Matrix

Priority Level Number	Severity Level	Priority Definition
1	Critical	Failure of a component where *one or more* people cannot perform critical business functions. Failure to complete this business function within 24 hours will have a negative financial impact on the company. No workaround is available, and degraded mode of operation is not available or not acceptable.
2	Urgent	Any of the following conditions is true: Failure of a component where *one or more* people cannot perform a critical business function. Failure to complete this business function within 24 hours will have a negative financial impact on the company. A workaround is available or a degraded mode of operation is available and acceptable. *or* Failure of a common component where *two or more* people cannot perform a critical business function. This failure will not have an immediate financial impact and there is no deadline within 5 days. No workaround is available and degraded mode of operation is not available. *or* Failure of a common component where *one or more* people cannot perform a critical business function and are at risk of not meeting a deadline for the critical business function in 5 days or less. There is no immediate financial impact. No workaround is available.
3	Important	Any of the following conditions is true: Failure of a component where *one person* cannot perform a critical business function. There is no workaround available. Failure of the business function will not have an immediate financial impact and there is no deadline of 5 days or less at risk. *or* Failure of a component where *one or more* people cannot perform a critical business function. None of the affected people has an immediate negative financial impact. One or more of the impacted people has a deadline of 5 days or less. A workaround is available or a degraded mode of operation is available and acceptable. *or* Failure of a component where *two or more* people cannot perform a critical business function. None of the impacted people has an immediate financial impact and none has a deadline of 5 days or less. A workaround is available or a degraded mode of operation is available and acceptable.

(continued)

Table 6–2   Service Center Priority Scheme and Definition Matrix (*Continued*)

Priority Level Number	Severity Level	Priority Definition
4	Low	Either of the following conditions is true: Failure of a component where *one person* cannot perform a critical business function. This failure will not have an immediate financial impact and there is no deadline within 5 days or less at risk. A workaround is available or a degraded mode of operation is available and acceptable. *or* Failure of a component that impacts a non-core business function, such as security or the health department.
5	Monitor	*No Business Impact.* Does not affect a core business function; for example, information requests and scheduled events.

The key goals in prioritizing requests are to

1. Implement unambiguous, easily understood priority ratings.

2. Make sure that all customers and IT personnel understand the priority ratings.

6.4.1 Priority Level

Priority levels are established based on overall impact to the business. When determining the priority to assign to a ticket, the agent must translate the caller's perception of the priority into the correct business priority level. This is a critical translation because the assigned priority level determines the target resolution time and the level of effort put forth by the service center. It will also establish the caller's expectation for resolution time. This can be a difficult task because the caller's perception of the priority is often higher than the agents. It is, therefore, extremely important to have very clear and well-defined priority levels so that agents select the correct priority and can clearly and confidently communicate the selection criteria to the caller. A sample service center priority level and definition matrix is shown in Table 6–2 and provides a description of each priority level.

6.4.2 Support for Priorities

The priority levels used by the service center must be understood and supported by callers, third-party support vendors, service center staff, and company management if they are to work correctly. Callers must realize that their incident, while critical to them, may be less critical to the business, and that service center resources are allocated based on business need. Third-party support vendors must understand and agree to support assigned priority levels within the same timeframe as the rest of the support center resources. Those terms would generally be documented in a service contract between the service center and the vendor. Internal company staff that support the service center must agree to provide the level of support required to meet the resolution times established in the priorities. This is particularly important for support resources that are not dedicated full time to the service center, such as a tier 3 support team. Often, the service center will develop internal service contracts, or service level agreements (SLAs), with those teams to ensure their commitment. Finally, company managers outside of the service center must give their full support to priority levels and not use rank to raise priority levels. A failure of any of these parties to understand and support the priorities can lead to misappropriation of limited resources and poor handling of high priority issues.

6.4.3 Setting Priorities

The responsibility for assigning priorities to a problem ultimately lies with the service center. The agent assigns the initial priority based on an understanding of the priority definitions and the caller's interpretation of the priority level. However, the priority can be changed at any time if further research or additional information warrants such a change. The priority can also change based on the passage of time if target resolution times are in jeopardy. A decision tree for determining priority is provided in Figure 6–4. This decision tree is based on the priorities described above. Realize that there are other approaches, one of which will be discussed in section 6.4.5.

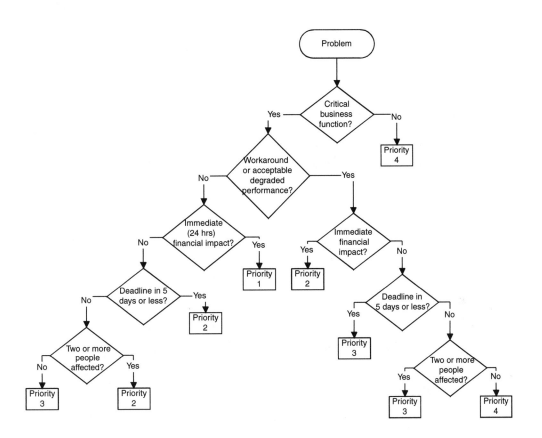

Figure 6–4 A decision tree for determining priority.

6.4.4 Priority Assignment for Problems

The service center establishes a priority hierarchy for problems, based primarily on the impact to the company's core business functions. The following list identifies other factors used in the evaluation:

- The number of users affected and the role of those users (i.e., core business function versus non-core business function).

- Whether service is completely shut down or degraded and whether a workaround is available.

A description of each of the priorities in Figure 6–4 follows.

Priority 1: Critical

For an incident to be rated as priority 1 (critical), three conditions must exist. First, it must impact a core business function, such as legal, accounting, risk management, finance, payroll, public relations, purchasing, tax, and so on. Second, an immediate workaround must not be available; that is, the impacted customers are essentially out of business. Finally, the incident impacts one or more customers such that a failure for that customer to complete some task in 24 hours will have a negative financial impact to the company.

For example, suppose the tax department has a filing due at noon on April 14 and their server crashes at 3:00 P.M. on April 13. Let's also assume that no workaround (such as a redundant backup) is available. Failure to file by noon on April 14 will result in penalties being assessed against the company by the IRS. This scenario meets all three criteria above. That is, it impacts a core business function (tax), there is no workaround available, and it definitely has an immediate financial impact (less than 24 hours). This incident would receive a priority 1 rating and the associated level of response from the service center.

Priority 2: Urgent

An incident can be prioritized as urgent in three different scenarios. In the first scenario, the incident impacts a critical business function and no immediate workaround is available. The incident impacts *at least one* and perhaps more customers, who have a deadline in 5 days or less, but there is no immediate financial impact. For example, suppose 4 days before payroll is due to be generated and sent to the payroll company, the payroll application ceases to function and there is no immediate workaround. This incident would be rated as priority level 2 because it is a critical business function, there is no workaround available, and it impacts work that must be done in 5 days or less.

In the second urgent scenario, the incident impacts *at least two people* in a critical business function, but no immediate workaround is available. The incident will not cause a negative financial impact in 24 hours or less. Further, no one affected has a deadline within 5 days. The key discriminator for this scenario is that it impacts two or more customers. For example, suppose three people in the tax department have a failure that causes them to lose print services. If upon questioning by the service center staff it is found that none of the three people is working on something that would have a negative financial impact if not completed within 24 hours and none of the three is working on anything with a deadline in 5 days or less, and, for whatever reason, an alternate printer is not available, then the incident should be rated as a level 2.

In the third urgent scenario, the incident impacts a critical business function, but a workaround is available. The condition that causes this incident to warrant a priority level of 2 is immediate financial impact. So, even though a workaround is available, the possibility of a negative financial impact in 24 hours or less means that the service center needs to place a high level of priority on this problem.

Priority 3: Important

An incident can be prioritized as important in three different scenarios. In each of the scenarios, the incident impacts a critical business function. In two of the scenarios, a workaround is available, and in the third scenario, a workaround is not available.

In the first scenario, the incident impacts a critical business function and no workaround is available. There is no risk of immediate financial impact and no deadline within the next 5 days. The condition that causes this incident to warrant a priority level of 3 instead of a priority level 2 is that *it only impacts one person*. If it impacted two or more people, and everything else remained the same, it would be classified as level 2, urgent. For example, assume a lawyer had a problem with Microsoft Word that prevented him from getting some task done, and there was no workaround available. Further, it is determined that he is not working on something where the failure to complete the task would have an immediate financial impact, and he has no deadline for this task or project in the next 5 days. Under these circumstances, the incident is prioritized as level 3, important.

In the second scenario, the incident impacts a critical business function, but a workaround *is* available. However, it is determined that there is a deadline of 5 days or less at risk. Under these conditions, the incident would receive a priority level of 3, important. Suppose a lawyer's printer stops working and he is working on something that is due in three days. Fortunately, he can attach to a second network printer on his floor, given instruction on how to do so from the service center, of course. Under these circumstances, his incident would receive a priority level of 3.

In the third scenario, the incident impacts a critical business scenario, but a workaround *is* available. In this scenario, there is no risk of an immediate financial impact and no deadline at risk in the next 5 days. The condition that causes this scenario to be prioritized as a 3 is that it impacts at least two people. If all other conditions remained the same, but the incident impacted only one person, it would be prioritized as level 4, low. Suppose something foul happens and four people lose access to email. Further, it is determined that the lack of email access will not have an immediate negative financial impact and does not put a deadline of 5 days or less at risk. Under these conditions, the incident would be prioritized as level 3.

Priority 4: Low

An incident is prioritized as a low priority in two different scenarios. In the first scenario, any incident that impacts a noncritical business function, such as the health department or the building security department, receives a low priority rating, no matter what the impact to the department. As an example, suppose the security department cannot get access to one of its computers. While this may severely impact their ability to conduct business, it would not warrant a priority level above low, because it is not a core business function.

In the second scenario, an incident impacts a critical business function, but either a workaround is available or a degraded mode of operation is available. It is determined that there is no risk of an immediate financial impact and no deadline of 5 days or less at risk. Finally, the incident impacts only one employee. (If the incident impacted two or more employees, it would be a level 3, as described above.) An example is a disruption in Internet access for an employee of a core business function, such as legal, but only when the requirement for access to the Internet does not impact the business (e.g., checking a nonbusiness related email account).

Incidents with low priority are handled on a first in/first out (FIFO) basis. In the examples given above, the service center would respond to the incident that was reported first.

Priority 5: Monitor

Incidents are categorized as level 5, monitor in two different cases. First, scheduled services, such as employee moves and changes and equipment upgrades, are prioritized as monitor. It is important for the service center to keep track of what is happening with items in this category, but they do not constitute an emergency. That is not to say that an incident won't become an emergency and then have its priority escalated. For example, if a scheduled server upgrade went afoul, then it would be entirely appropriate for its priority to be escalated up from monitor.

Second, an incident that formerly had a higher priority rating may be downgraded to monitor for some predefined period of time. If, for example, a server has a recurring problem and is fixed yet again, the service center may decide, rather than close the ticket, to leave the ticket open for some number of days, but in a status of monitor.

6.4.5 Other Factors Used in Prioritizing an Incident

The factors used above for prioritizing an incident are primarily related to a particular customer and that customer's situation. However, in addition to those factors, it is also important to consider factors that impact elements of the infrastructure that are not necessarily related to specific internal customers.

For example, if one of your company's Internet sites is down and it does not impact anyone internally or have an immediate financial impact, it could have a serious impact on the company's image. For instance, if a content server that presents the company to the public receives 8,000 hits per day were to malfunction, the company could receive bad press.

Suppose, for example, a common component fails and impacts 10 people, none of whom is working on something that will have an immediate financial impact or a deadline in 5 days or less, and a workaround is available. Strictly following the definitions above and the decision tree, this incident should be prioritized at level 3, important. However, because 10 people are affected, the service center may elect to raise the priority to a level 2. If even more employees were affected, the service center could raise the priority to level 1.

Judgment must always be exercised when prioritizing incidents. Another example where the service center may consider raising a priority level is when some deadline is very close and an incident occurs. Suppose an employee is making a presentation to senior level management in 20 minutes and his or her laptop, which contains the presentation, won't boot up. Following the decision tree, this would be prioritized as a level 2, urgent (it is a critical business function, no workaround, no immediate financial impact, deadline in 5 days or less). Given that there were no other priority 1 incidents, the service center should rate this incident as priority 1 and help this customer as quickly as possible.

One point to keep in mind if you do take the approach, as in the example above, of raising a priority level to help a customer, is that your metrics will be skewed. From the perspective of metrics, you would be better off to rate the ticket, as a priority 2, but dispatch a team immediately. Remember, the initial response times represent the longest amount of time it should take to make the initial contact. There is nothing that says you can't respond sooner. This approach allows you to both help the customer more quickly and retain valid metrics.

The decision tree in Figure 6–4 overlooks an important consideration. Suppose an entire site of users were unable to connect to ACCTPRD9 due to a database server outage. Because of the number of customers impacted, they would receive immediate attention. However, a single user without access to the database server would not, in most circumstances, receive immediate attention. An exception should be when the single user, such as the database administrator, is critical to the operation of the ACCTPRD9.

Service that is slower than usual but still available may receive a lower priority than the complete failure of some component. In this case, the operational status may only be considered degraded. If a business-critical function cannot be performed (e.g., printing tax documents on April 13), immediate attention to resolve the problem may take precedence. A deciding factor may be the occurrence of a problem at a critical time, forcing a higher priority level than would be assigned at a less critical time.

The service center's priority matrix is used as a guideline for assigning priority levels; however, ultimate assignment of priority is made at the discretion of the service center staff, the caller, and a service center technician (if applicable) by considering each individual circumstance.

6.4.6 Priority Assignments for Services

Services (as opposed to problems) requested by customers are recorded and tracked, as are all other calls into the service center. Tracking all requests may indicate when new requirements or additional services may be required. Special consideration is given to requests of a critical nature (e.g., "As a security measure, please..."). Priorities assigned to requests for service are assigned at the discretion of the service center and the caller, but are generally assigned as level 5, monitor. In other words, these are work orders and should be tracked to make sure they are completed and closed. However, the priority should be raised automatically when the service center is at risk of missing its target delivery dates and times.

6.4.7 Changing Priority Levels

Priority levels may be changed for one or more of the following reasons:

- Priority may have been entered in error.
- Priority may have escalated due to passage of time (e.g., a function has been down for an extended or unacceptable time, or an issue has had no activity for an extended or unacceptable time).
- The priority may have decreased due to restored but degraded service or temporary workaround.
- The caller, agent, or technician has expressed a reasonable exception to the normal level of priority

Flexibility is essential to successfully managing the priority of problems, questions, and requests. Most important, the service center must responsibly assess each individual call and assign the proper priority level according to the needs of the customer and corporate community.

6.4.8 Implementing Priorities

Once you have established new priority levels, train the service center staff on the use and assignment of the new levels. Provide different scenarios to make sure the staff understands how you expect calls to be prioritized. Publish the new priority levels for the entire customer base. You may want to consider a marketing campaign to make sure all customers understand how priorities are determined.

If you are combining help desks, you should consider testing the new priority levels prior to their implementation. This will verify that the new priority scheme will work for both help desks and will provide training for all of the staff.

6.4.9 Alternative Priority Schemes

There are many alternatives to the priority scheme shown above. Many successful service center managers believe that simpler is better, and therefore only use three or four priority levels (as opposed to the five shown above). The fewer the priority levels, the greater the distinction between each, and thus the more easily they are understood and applied by all. That said, there are other successful centers that use a seemingly more complex approach by utilizing both priority and severity, applying both characteristics to each ticket.

Service centers that use both priority and severity segregate between response time and impact to the customer or business, respectively. The priority assigned determines the initial response times required and is based on the selected impact to the customer. This approach allows you to have high severity and high priority issues as expected, but it also allows you to have high priority/low severity and low priority/high severity cases as well. An example of this scheme is shown in Tables 6–3 and 6–4.

Suppose, for example, that the accounting department collects invoicing information from remote servers on the fifth of each month and then generates invoices on the sixth. On the eighth, someone in accounting notices that he cannot connect to one of the remote servers. The impact to this customer is critical; he cannot conduct important business. The priority, on the other hand, can be a very low 5, with a target resolution in 1 week. Even with the low priority, there is ample time to resolve the problem before it impacts the customer.

Table 6–3 Severity Scale

Severity	Customer Impact
Critical	Customer cannot conduct important business.
Impaired	Customer's ability to conduct important business impaired but functioning.
Monitor	Customer has a problem, but nothing important is impacted.

Table 6–4 Priority Scale

Priority	Initial Response	Target Resolution
1	Immediate	2 hours
2	30 minutes	4 hours
3	2 hours	8 hours
4	6 hours	24 hours
5	1 day	1 week

It is possible that a service center will use more than one scheme to prioritize tickets. This is the case when different service plans are offered to customers. Some customers may want a deluxe service plan with faster response times, while others choose the more economical basic service plan. Generally, when different priority schemes are used within the same service center, different teams use them. In other words, team A may handle all of the deluxe customers and team B and C handle the basic customers. In this way, one team does not use more than one priority scheme. This is important, since it can be difficult enough to implement a single scheme successfully.

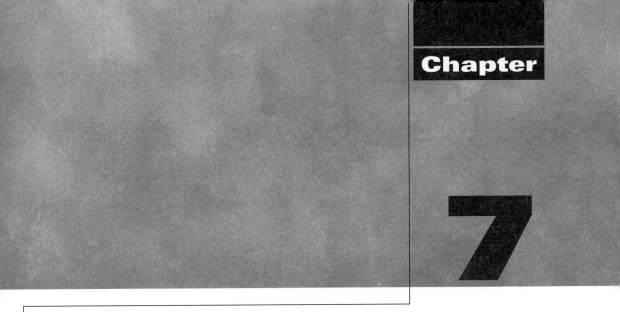

Service Delivery

The service delivery process is initiated following the problem logging process, as shown in Figure 7–1. Once the customer has been validated and the problem logged, the service center must provide some solution for the request. The service delivery process can be subdivided into two core processes: problem determination and work restoration. First, service center agents must use processes and techniques to gather enough information to determine the cause of the problem. Once the problem is uncovered, agents can develop a strategy to resolve it. The strategy may involve testing one or more solutions and then applying the correct one. The problem is not considered resolved until the customer accepts the proposed solution.

Solving the problem and delivering the final solution (a process called *work restoration*) may be beyond the capability or problem-solving time limits of the tier 1 agent. When this occurs, the agent must escalate or route the problem to another resource pool.

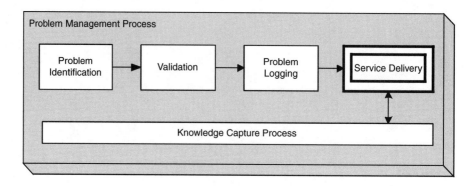

Figure 7–1 The service delivery process follows the problem logging process.

▶ 7.1 Problem Determination

The goal of the problem determination process is to gather enough information to identify the underlying problem the customer is experiencing. Customers usually report the symptoms, not the cause, of the problem they are experiencing. To eliminate the troublesome symptoms, the service center must find the solution to the underlying problem.

Often, the reported symptoms will be familiar enough to the agent that he or she will know the underlying problem and can quickly implement a solution. The symptoms are usually gathered during the logging process so that the agent can categorize and prioritize the ticket. If it is not a familiar problem, the agent must gather additional information.

Gathering the additional information requires interaction between the agent and the customer. The interaction may be over the phone or via electronic communications. In either case, the agent must ask questions that identify what the customer was trying to do that couldn't be done and the environmental conditions that existed at the time the problem occurred.

To eliminate the symptoms the customer is experiencing, the underlying problem must be discovered. As mentioned, the symptoms may be so common that the problem is immediately identified. In other cases, the symptoms are not familiar, so the agents must begin problem solving. The exception to this occurs when the sources identifying the problem are monitoring tools. If your service center is set up so that tickets can be generated automatically by monitoring tools, then the monitoring tools should report only problems, not symptoms. The use of thresholds and event correlation software should eliminate or filter out symptoms and ensure that tickets are generated only for true problems or potential problems (being proactive).

Identifying the underlying problem is an iterative process. The agent works with the customer to systematically identify and eliminate the possible underlying causes of the problem. The process continues until the problem is resolved, and it may involve one or more service center agents. The first task for the agent is to determine what the customer was trying to accomplish and then what kept the customer from doing it. While this sounds obvious, it is often the case that the customer tells you only the symptom or only part of what he or she was trying to accomplish. Problem solving should not proceed until the agent has clarified the true problem. An agent can waste a lot of time attempting to resolve a symptom instead of the problem.

Once the problem has been clarified, the agent may know the solution. If not, he or she needs to gather other information that might be related to the problem, such as the environmental conditions. Beyond the obvious items, such as the customer's hardware and software, the agent should find out what other applications were running at the time the problem occurred. The agent should find out if the problem has occurred before, if it happens consistently, if it can be re-created, if the user has reported the problem previously, and what the user has done to fix or work around the problem. The agent must gather all the related information and attempt to filter out unnecessary details.

If the service center agent has remote control tools, he or she can very quickly gather all of this information. Using the tools is particularly helpful when the customer is not very technically savvy and may have difficulty answering the agent's questions. With remote control, the agent can gather the information directly, relying less on the customer. This is an extremely productive approach when the agents have the tools, know how to use them, and have permission from the customer.

Once the information has been gathered, the agent may recognize the problem and may know the solution. If the agent recognizes the problem and a solution is available, the agent should apply the solution and verify that it actually fixed the customer's problem. If the customer is satisfied, the agent closes the ticket. If the tested solution does not fix the problem or no solutions are available, the agent may need to ask more questions and the process begins again (see Figure 7–2). If the problem is new to the agent and the solution is not known, the agent must take some other action to find a solution.

Agents will inevitably encounter problems that they do not recognize. After they have identified and documented what the customer was attempting to do, what was expected to occur, what actually occurred, and all the related environmental information, agents should check the knowledge base for documentation of the same, or a similar, problem. If knowledge base reports (KBRs) are found, the agent identifies the subset of reports that are most likely to resolve the problem. The agent must then iterate through the reports until a solution is found and accepted by the customer. If none of the KBRs fix the problem or no reports are found, the agent must take some other action.

Assuming the agent has documented the problem, does not recognize the problem or a solution, and cannot find the problem or its solution in the knowledge base, he or she must develop a list of the possible causes, possible solutions, and related assumptions. The agent should iterate through the list of possible problems, eliminating them from the list when they are disproved, eventually ending up with a short list of possibilities. Once the short list is created, the agent should verify all assumptions and test possible solutions. At any point, the agent may require additional information that he or she can get from the customer or can gather directly by using a remote control tool. Hopefully, this approach will lead to the solution, which the agent can apply and the customer will accept. Once the customer accepts the solution, the agent should start the knowledge base process to capture the new problem, symptoms, solution, and other pertinent information.

The problem-solving process just discussed is shown in Figure 7–2. It shows that the agent starts the process by clarifying the problem and gathering all the environmental information that may be related to the problem. When this task is accomplished, the agent may recognize the problem and know the solution. If not, the agent proceeds to search the knowledge base. If the problem or solution, or both, are not found, then the agent must develop a list of possible causes and solutions, and then iterate through those until the correct solution is found.

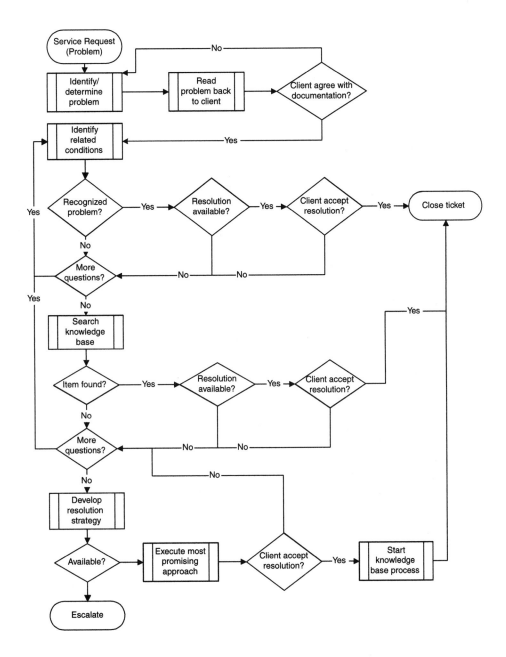

Figure 7–2 An approach to the problem-solving process.

▶ 7.2 Work Restoration

After determining and documenting the problem, the work restoration process begins. To return service as quickly as possible to the client, it may be necessary to provide the customer with a problem bypass. A problem bypass, or workaround, is a partial or complete circumvention of a problem prior to final resolution of the problem. Problem bypass varies, depending on the type of problem. For example, if the problem is a server down, then a hot backup server may already be in place and the customer may not have even noticed that his or her server was down—the bypass occurred automatically. Other problems may have simple workarounds available that are documented in the knowledge base. In these cases, the customer is provided with a workaround so they can continue to work until the root problem is resolved. A typical example is that a customer's default network printer is down, so they are instructed on how to use a different network printer until their printer is repaired.

Work restoration is the process the service center implements to resolve customer problems. It requires that agents clarify problems and then find and apply solutions or workarounds. A service center needs to establish processes to ensure that agents take all of the necessary steps to resolve the customer's problem, and then document that knowledge for the benefit of all other users. In a multitier service center model, defining the work restoration process is even more important because tickets are passed from tier to tier and group to group. This is important to ensure that agents take all the necessary steps prior to escalating the problem to another agent. Not only do work restoration processes need to be developed for each tier, thorough escalation procedures must be included as well.

Eliminating customer problems is often a difficult task because the customer environment has become very complex. Resolving problems in this complex environment often requires specialized expertise, cooperation, and assistance spanning multiple disciplines. To provide that expertise efficiently, many service centers are organized using a multitiered organization model. The multitiered model, with specialized pools of expertise at each tier level, is efficient for maximizing expert resource utilization, but can actually increase the difficulty of resolving a given problem, because the structure adds complexity to the problem-solving process.

The work restoration process currently used in many service centers is ineffective. Only a limited number of problems can be resolved at tier 1. This is a result of too little expertise at tier 1, lack of a knowledge base to work from, and too many tasks owned by tiers 2 and 3. As a result, many items are escalated. Items that are escalated or routed take longer to resolve and often end with the tier 1 and tier 2 agents spending time gathering the same information. To make matters worse, it is often the case that in many service centers, every item escalated to a tier 2 desktop software group results in a dispatch to the customer's desk. This of course is extremely inefficient and wastes a lot of time spent traveling.

To effectively manage the multitier model, a service center must define problem-solving responsibilities at each tier and must have well defined procedures that describe when and how problems should be routed or escalated between tiers. A service center must also establish which problems and services each tier is expected to resolve (a concept called *ownership*) and where to route that problem when the intended tier cannot resolve the problem.

All of these problems can be overcome by implementing better processes and tools, providing training, and defining tier-level responsibilities. The work restoration process is subdivided into series of steps that repeat until the problem is resolved or a bypass has been provided to the customer. The processes defined in the following sections are for a multitiered service center with multiple pools of expertise available at tier 2 and tier 3. Moving a service request from one tier to the next is referred to as *escalation* and typically occurs when one tier does all the work they can do and there is still work to be done. Many people choose to refer to this routine, predefined escalation as *routing* and only use the term escalation to refer to nonroutine escalations (such as a customer requesting to speak to a manager). Many service centers have predefined a subset of problems that are automatically escalated (routed) to tier 2, without the tier 1 agent attempting to resolve the problem. A typical example is hardware support, which is often outsourced.

The following sections discuss in detail the problem determination and work restoration process steps, prioritizing service requests, escalation procedures, service center tiers, resource pools within each tier, and responsibilities at each tier.

The key objectives in work restoration are to

1. Provide a solution to the root cause of the problem as quickly as possible.
2. Provide a workaround solution as quickly as possible if a repair for the root cause is not available.
3. Resolve as many problems as possible during the initial contact (at tier 1) with the customer.
4. Route or escalate as few problems as possible.
5. Minimize the number of problems escalated to tier 3 agents.
6. Dispatch tier 2 agents only when the problem cannot be resolved remotely.

7.2.1 Tier 1 Service Center Problem-Solving Process

The problem-solving process in Figure 7–2 is used again in Figures 7–3, 7–4, and 7–5, but it has been augmented with escalation procedures. As the illustrations show, the problem-solving process is essentially the same, no matter which agent at which tier is trying to solve a problem. The difference comes in when the agent solving the problem has done all that he or she can to solve the problem and there is still work to be done. The additional escalation steps and considerations are indicated with heavy black lines. Escalation usually occurs under five circumstances.

1. The agent has reached a predefined time limit and must pass the problem to someone else.
2. The problem is beyond the skill level of the agent.
3. The problem resolution requires security rights that the agent does not have.
4. The priority and nature of the problem requires the agent to forward the problem to a specialist or a priority-handling team.
5. The customer has requested that the problem be escalated.

As Figure 7–3 illustrates, when a customer request comes into the service center and is categorized as a problem, the service center must identify and resolve the problem. Agents may be very familiar with the problem and may also know the solution. If it is not a common problem, the agents should search the knowledge base to find a matching KBR. In either case, the agent recognized the problem or found a matching KBR, he or she must determine if a resolution is available. The resolution may be known or documented in the KBR. If known or found, the agent provides the resolution to the customer. The customer tries the resolution and either accepts it, in which case the agent closes the ticket, or does not accept it, in which case the agent must go back to the knowledge base and continue searching for applicable KBRs or continue trying resolutions (if more than one was available on the original KBR).

If no resolutions are found or known, the agent should check to see if the same problem or a similar one was previously escalated for resolution. If it is a common, recurring problem without a resolution, most agents will know this and should inform the customer that someone has been assigned (hopefully) to fix it. The agent should also tell the customer when the service center will contact him or her with a status update and the target resolution date, if known. For example, it may be a known bug that will be fixed in the next release of the software due out in August. If the customer accepts this situation, then the ticket is updated to set a tickler and kept open. If the customer does not accept this situation, the ticket and the customer are escalated to the appropriate predefined manager.

If the knowledge base was searched and a KBR was not found, then the problem is a new problem for the service center and the agent begins analysis and troubleshooting. The agent continues to collect information and explore the conditions around the symptoms in an effort to isolate the problem. If the agent has gathered all of the data required to understand the problem but is still unable to provide a resolution, then the agent should seek permission from the customer to take remote control of the PC, if remote control tools are available. If a resolution still cannot be found, then the agent should escalate the problem to tier 2. If a resolution is found, then the agent must determine if a new KBR is required. If it is required, then the agent should proceed to the knowledge base process. If a new report is not required, then an existing report probably needs to be updated with the new symptoms that were not found during the original search of the knowledge base.

If the customer accepts the resolution, the ticket is closed. If the customer does not accept the resolution, the agent returns once more to the knowledge base or continues troubleshooting. If the agent has diligently and thoroughly searched the knowledge base and has performed the appropriate troubleshooting but has not found a resolution, the problem should be escalated to the appropriate tier 2 resource pool.

There are a couple of risks in this process that the service center manager or a shift manager must carefully monitor. In the case where a problem is common, the process allows the agent to skip searching the knowledge base. This is allowed for the sake of speed. The risk, though, is that if a new resolution has become available, the agent may not know about it because he or she has not reviewed the KBR. The second risk is that the agent may get in the habit of skipping the knowledge base. This could lead to problems being unnecessarily escalated, or the agent may waste time troubleshooting a problem that has already been resolved. The service center manager or shift manager must gather metrics to monitor the use of the knowledge base.

7.2.2 Tier 2 Service Center Problem-Solving Process

The first thing that a tier 2 agent must do is review the initial response time commitment made to the customer. This allows the agent to prioritize his or her work so that the service center meets its customer commitments. The agent is responsible for achieving that commitment. Once the agent understands the commitment, he or she must review the ticket, then check to see if the problem has been previously identified. This is an important step to ensure that the agent doesn't begin to troubleshoot a problem that someone else is already working on. If the agent finds that the problem has been previously identified, then the agent should inform the customer that someone is working on the problem but it has not yet been resolved. If the customer accepts that position, the agent updates the ticket and keeps it open. The customer may not accept that position, in which case the customer and the ticket should be escalated to the appropriate manager.

How the tier 2 agent finds out if the problem has been previously identified varies by service center. In Figure 7–4, this step occurs immediately after the tier 2 agent reviews the ticket. The agent can stop work immediately if he or she discovers or knows that someone else is already assigned and working on the problem. In smaller tier 2 resource pools, it is possible that all the agents in the pool know what everyone else is working on. If they don't know, then how does an agent find out? Many resource pools keep a list of problems they are working on, the associated plan for completing the work, the name of the agent assigned, and other helpful information so that the manager of that resource pool can keep track of the work on his or her plate. If the pool maintains a list of these assigned problems, then all agents can review the list to see if the problem has been previously identified.

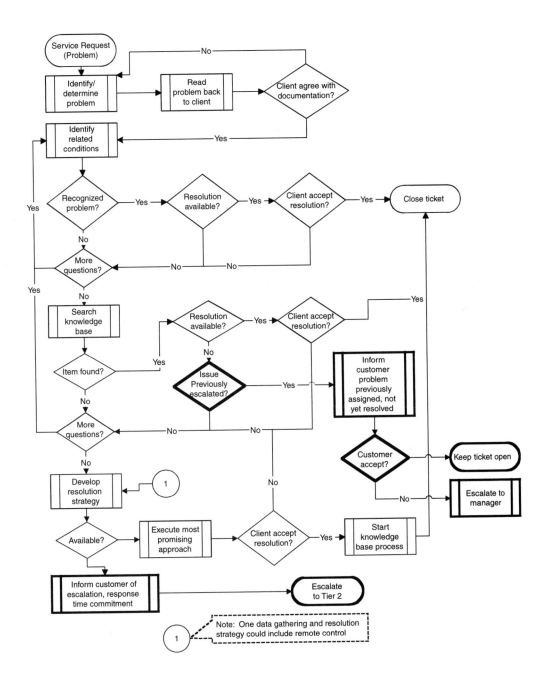

Figure 7–3   Tier 1 problem-solving approach with escalation.

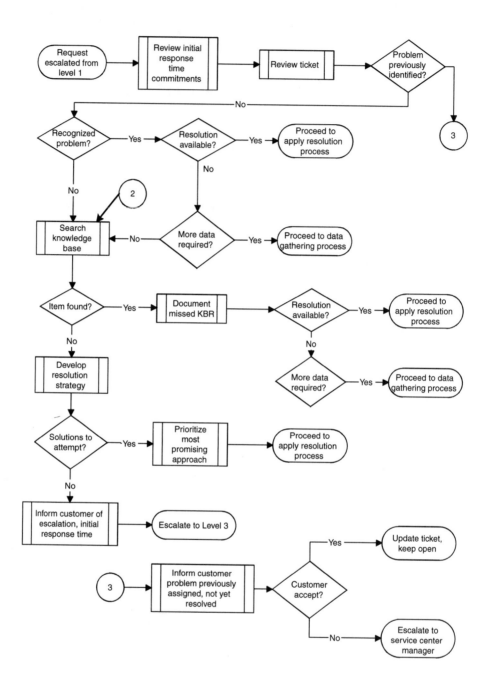

Figure 7–4 Tier 2 problem-solving approach with escalation.

Some service centers build a knowledge base report for each new problem, even if the problem has not yet been resolved. This is a good approach because it allows all service center agents to see that the problem has been previously identified and that someone is already responsible for finding a solution. In this scenario, the knowledge base is the communication device. For service centers that use this approach, the tier 2 problem-solving diagram would be slightly different than the one shown in Figure 7–4. The "Problem previously identified?" diamond would be eliminated. The agent would search the knowledge base and find a matching report that does not have a resolution but a note that someone else is assigned to the problem and is working on it. The agent would notify the customer and stop working on the problem. This approach is shown in Figure 7–5.

Back to the tier 2 problem-solving process. After the agent understands the response time commitments and reviews the ticket, he or she may recognize the problem, even though the tier 1 agent did not. If the tier 2 agent recognizes the problem and a solution is available, he or she proceeds to the apply resolution process. If the problem is recognized but a solution is not available, the agent can either search the knowledge base or gather more data. The agent's choice depends to some extent on what the tier 1 agent did prior to escalating the ticket. The ticket may show that the tier 1 agent thoroughly searched the knowledge base and did not find a matching report. The ticket may also show that the tier 1 agent did *not* thoroughly search the knowledge base, so the tier 2 agent may decide to perform his own search before gathering additional data. If the tier 2 agent believes that the tier 1 agent conducted a thorough search of the knowledge base, he or she should proceed to the data gathering process.

If the tier 2 agent searches the knowledge base with the information the tier 1 agent documented in the ticket and finds the correct KBR, that fact should be captured, which is shown as "Document missed KBR" in the process diagram. It is a valuable metric to capture. If a tier 2 agent finds the solution in a KBR, using the same information as the tier 1 agent, you need to figure out why the ticket was escalated. Does the tier 1 agent need additional training on how to search the knowledge base? Was the tier 1 agent forced to escalate the ticket because he or she ran out of time? Did the tier 1 agent bother to search the knowledge base, or did he or she simply escalate the ticket? These are important issues for you to monitor. Gathering these metrics could indicate a problem with a particular agent or perhaps with the knowledge base in general. If many tier 1 agents are not finding KBRs, then perhaps the there are many "bad" reports in the system, or perhaps the system is too slow. You should take corrective action to keep your tier 1 resolution rates up. Further, most tier 2 agents become very frustrated when a problem that should have and could have been resolved at tier 1 becomes their responsibility. Morale and mutual respect can suffer.

If the tier 2 agent finds a matching KBR and a solution is available, he or she proceeds to the apply resolution process. If the agent finds a matching report but a solution is not available, the agent may need to gather additional data to clarify the problem and search the knowledge base again.

If the agent has gathered as much data as possible, has thoroughly clarified the problem, thoroughly searched the knowledge base, and no matching report was found, then the agent is facing a new problem and must develop a resolution strategy. The resolution strategy is the sum of all the ideas the agent has on how to solve the problem, based on the given data. When problem solving, most people have a list of things to try and a list of assumptions. The agent should document and prioritize both, and then systematically validate or eliminate assumptions. The agent may seek permission to make a site visit or use remote control tools, if available. He or she should then proceed to the *apply resolution process* (described in the next section) with each of the possible solutions, trying each until the problem is solved. If after trying each solution, the problem is not fixed, the agent should inform the customer that the problem will be escalated to tier 3 and what the initial response time will be from the tier 3 agent.

Apply Resolution Process

This subprocess is initiated when an agent has a resolution for the customer. If remote control tools are available, the agent should get permission from the customer and then take remote control of the customer's machine. Then the agent applies or executes the solution remotely. If the customer accepts the solution, then the agent should start the knowledge base process, if necessary, and then close the customer's ticket. If the customer does not accept the solution or the solution doesn't work, then the agent should initiate the data gathering process, described next.

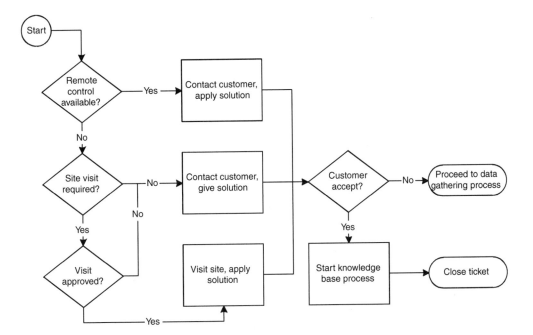

Figure 7-5 The apply resolution process.

If remote control tools are not available, then the agent must decide if a site visit is required to apply the solution. If it is not required, the agent must contact the customer (by telephone, email, fax) and step him or her through the resolution steps. If the customer accepts the solution, the agent should start the knowledge base process, if necessary, and then close the customer's ticket. If the customer does not accept the solution or the solution doesn't work, then the agent should initiate the data gathering process.

If remote control tools are not available and a site visit is required to apply the solution, the agent should get permission from a manager to be dispatched. If the agent gets permission, then he or she visits the site and applies the solution. If the manager does not permit the site visit, the agent must contact the customer and step him or her through the resolution steps. In either case, if the customer accepts the solution, the agent should start the knowledge base process, if necessary, and then close the customer's ticket. If the customer does not accept the solution or the solution doesn't work, then the agent should initiate the data gathering process.

The site visit approval step is included in the process, but may not be required in all circumstances. For example, hardware problems will nearly always require a site visit. If your service center has a tier 2 resource pool dedicated to hardware support, then agents may not be required to seek approval from the manager. The intent of this step is to prevent habitual dispatch. If you are attempting to break the cycle of agents automatically visiting the customer's desktop to troubleshoot and apply solutions, this step is a control mechanism that can help you "retrain" agents. It may be required for only a few months, or it may need to be a permanent part of your process.

Data-Gathering Process

Figure 7–6 illustrates the data-gathering process. This subprocess is initiated when an agent requires more data to solve the customer's problem. If remote control tools are available, the agent should get permission from the customer and then take remote control of the customer's machine. Then the agent gathers the data remotely and may require little input from the customer. When the agent has gathered enough additional data, he or she returns to the tier 2 problem-solving approach and searches the knowledge base, using the new information.

If remote control tools are not available, then the agent must decide if a site visit is required to gather additional information. If it is not required, the agent must contact the customer with a set of questions to gather the additional data required. When the agent has gathered enough additional data, he or she returns to the tier 2 problem-solving approach and searches the knowledge base, using the new information.

If remote control tools are not available and a site visit is required to gather additional data, the agent should get permission for the visit from a manager. If the agent gets permission, then he or she visits the site and gathers additional data. If the manager does not permit the site visit, the agent must contact the customer to ask new questions. When the agent has gathered enough additional data, he or she returns to the tier 2 problem-solving approach and searches the knowledge base, using the new information. If the agent is at the customer site, he or she may be able to access the knowledge base directly from the customer's machine. If not, the agent may develop a resolution strategy and attempt solutions at the customer's site.

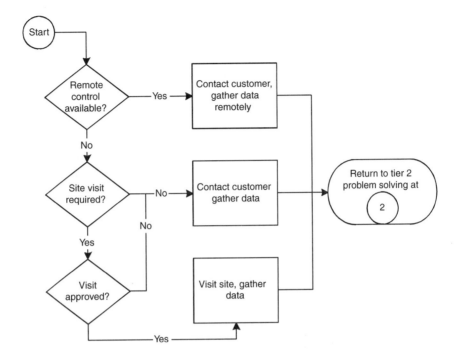

Figure 7–6 The data-gathering process.

7.2.3 Tier 3 Service Center Problem-Solving Process

The tier 3 process, shown in Figure 7–7, is very similar to the tier 2 process, but there are some differences that should be discussed. The first thing that a tier 3 agent must do is review the initial response time commitment made to the customer. This allows the agent to prioritize his or her work so that the service center meets its customer commitments. The agent is responsible for achieving that commitment. Once the agent understands the commitment, he or she must review the ticket.

After the agent understands the response time commitments and reviews the ticket, he or she may recognize the problem, even though the tier 2 agent did not. If the tier 3 agent recognizes the problem and a solution is available, he or she proceeds to the apply resolution process. If the problem is recognized but a solution is not available, the agent can either search the knowledge base or gather more data. The agent's choice depends to some extent on what the tier 2 agent did prior to escalating the ticket. The ticket may show that the tier 2 agent thoroughly searched the knowledge base and did not find a matching report. The ticket may also show that the tier 2 agent did *not* thoroughly search the knowledge base, so the tier 3 agent may decide to perform his own search before attempting to gather additional data. If the tier 3 agent believes that the tier 2 agent conducted a thorough search of the knowledge base, he or she should proceed to the data gathering process.

If the tier 3 agent searches the knowledge base with the information the tier 1 and tier 2 agents documented in the ticket and finds the correct KBR, that fact should be captured, which is shown as "Document missed KBR" in the process diagram. It is a valuable metric to capture. If a tier 3 agent finds the solution in a KBR, using the same information as the tier 1 and/or 2 agent, you need to figure out why the ticket was escalated. Does the tier 1 or 2 agent need additional training on how to search the knowledge base? Was the tier 1 or 2 agent forced to escalate the ticket because he or she ran out of time? Did the tier 1 or 2 agent bother to search the knowledge base, or did he or she simply escalate the ticket? These are important issues for you to monitor. Gathering these metrics could indicate a problem with a particular agent or perhaps with the knowledge base in general. If many tier 1 or 2 agents are not finding KBRs, then perhaps there are many bad reports in the system or perhaps it is too slow. You should take corrective action to keep your tier 1 and 2 resolution rates up. As mentioned about tier 2 agents, most tier 3 agents become very frustrated when a problem that should have and could have been resolved at tier 1 or 2 becomes their responsibility. Morale and mutual respect can suffer.

If the tier 3 agent finds a matching KBR and a solution is available, he or she proceeds to the apply resolution process. If the agent finds a matching report but a solution is not available, the agent may need to gather additional data to clarify the problem and search the knowledge base again.

If the agent has gathered as much data as possible, has thoroughly clarified the problem, thoroughly searched the knowledge base, and no matching report was found, then the agent is facing a new problem and must develop a resolution strategy. The resolution strategy is the sum of all the ideas the agent has on how to solve the problem, based on the given data. When problem solving, most people have a list of things to try and a list of assumptions. The agent should document and prioritize both, and then systematically validate or eliminate assumptions.

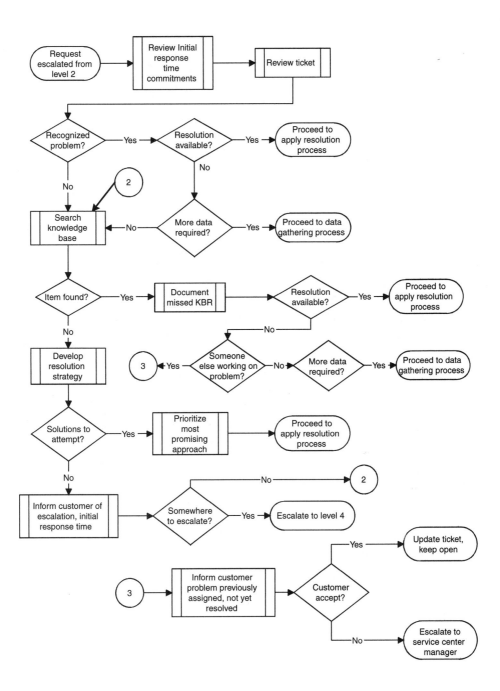

Figure 7–7 Tier 3 problem-solving approach with escalation.

The agent may seek permission to make a site visit or use remote control tools, if available. The agent should then proceed to the apply resolution process with each of the possible solutions, trying each until the problem is solved. If after trying each solution, the problem is not fixed, what occurs next depends on your organization and the type of problem. In the case of a tier 3 agent, there may be no one else to escalate the problem to. If this is the case, the tier 3 agent should notify the pool owner. In some cases, tier 3 could escalate certain problems to the appropriate vendors or in-house development teams (if they are not already considered tier 3). Prior to escalating, the agent must update the ticket and either the agent or the help desk must inform the customer of the escalation and when the initial response should be received by the tier 3 resource. If there is no where else to escalate the ticket, then the tier 3 resource pool continues attempting to resolve the problem by starting the process over again. This may require the team to research many different sources, including the Internet, chat forums, and so on. The agent should inform the customer what will happen next, and if possible, give the customer a time commitment.

7.2.4 Customer Follow-up

All service centers should consider implementing a policy to follow up with customers after a ticket is closed. This is an excellent way to generate goodwill by showing the customers that the service center cares. The service center should check to see if the problem has truly been resolved or if the customer is still experiencing problems. Further, the service center needs to tell the customer how to reopen the ticket should the problem recur. It is important to reopen the ticket as opposed to creating a new ticket when the same problem recurs. Reopening the ticket indicates that the problem may not have been resolved correctly in the first place. If this is the case, then someone must find the real solution and may need to update a knowledge base report so that the "bad" solution is not propagated. It may also indicate that testing of the original solution was not adequately performed.

For follow-up to be effective, it should occur within a few days of the incident closure. Follow-up contact does not have to be—in fact, should not be—a lengthy process. The shorter the better for both the service center and the customer. You really only need to ask if the solution worked and if the customer is satisfied with the solution. You may also ask if the customer is satisfied with the service center. As mentioned, you should provide the customer with instructions on how to reopen the ticket, if necessary. The follow-up contact can occur in several different ways. Many service centers have one person who is designated to provide all of the follow-up contact. Another approach is to have the original owner of the ticket follow up with the customer. This is a nice touch but requires that the tier 1 agents have time to conduct follow-up work. A third approach is to create a pool of required follow-up contacts and assign groups to share the responsibility, in addition to their normal service center responsibilities. This is a good approach too, because it makes customer follow-up and satisfaction everyone's responsibility. A final approach is to send an email as a follow-up. While this lacks the personal touch, it makes up for it in other ways. First, it does not increase the workload of service center agents. The email can be generated automatically when the ticket status is changed to closed. Summary information from the ticket and even the SLA can be added automatically, showing the service center's performance. Instructions on how to reopen the ticket, or a reopen button, can be added automatically. A reference to the online database can be provided so customers can help themselves next time, if necessary. Finally, you can ask customers for feedback on their service center experience by placing some satisfaction-level buttons on an attached form. The user clicks one of no more than five buttons indicating the level of satisfaction with the service center. Wouldn't it be terrific to have satisfaction feedback from the customer on every closed incident?

▶ 7.3 Service Center Organization Overview

The organization of the service center determines where and how items are escalated and routed. Many internal service centers use, and will continue to use, a three-tiered organizational structure to provide response to service requests. The resource pools within each tier are relatively small, and typically, each successive tier has more expertise in a specific area than the previous tier. Generally, when items are escalated they move to a pool, not to a specific individual.

The key objectives in service center organization are to

1. Ensure that each service center escalation pool clearly understands their service center responsibilities.

2. Ensure that each service center escalation pool clearly understands their initial response time commitments.

3. Ensure that each service center escalation pool clearly understands where to escalate items should escalation be warranted.

4. Ensure that the service center escalation pool manager clearly understands his or her responsibilities and commitments.

7.3.1 Multiple Help Desks

Many companies have multiple internal help desks, as illustrated in Figure 7–8. For example, there may be one help desk that supports internal corporate headquarter customers, a second help desk at a different location that supports a corporate subsidiary, a third help desk that supports the wide area network, a fourth help desk for telecommunications, and so on. This setup is characteristic of evolution, not design. As applications and systems become more distributed and more and more information is shared between corporate and its business units, it becomes increasingly difficult to find the correct owner of a particular problem. Help desks in these environments are under increasing pressure to cooperate and resolve problems. As the users' environments begin to appear and act more homogeneous, help desks and service centers serving those customers must adapt to those changes. These help desks and service centers must operate as one virtual service center to satisfy customers. Although politics and "turf" will probably be obstacles, it would certainly be in the best interest of all the help desks involved to take the time to organize themselves as a single virtual help desk or service center. This can be accomplished by taking action jointly to accomplish the four goals listed above.

If you can get beyond basic cooperation, there are many other benefits to be had on a corporate-wide basis. One center can provide after-hours support for all of the help desks. The corporation could leverage buying power to purchase common support tools, allowing for simplified data sharing. If all customers called the same number, an automatic call distribution (ACD) could route calls to a large virtual pool of resources. According to queuing theory, this would be a much more efficient use of resources. Trained resources from one business unit could take overflow calls from another and provide equally good service. The customer would never know. If specialized expertise is required, it can come from anywhere in the entire corporate structure. Calls requiring dispatch can easily be routed to the correct resource pool at the correct site. The potential benefits to customers across the entire corporation are significant.

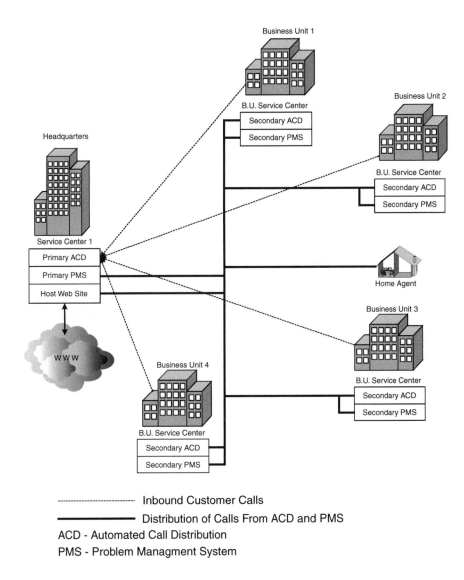

Figure 7–8 Multisite virtual service center.

▶ 7.4 Escalation

Escalation is the process of transferring responsibility for resolving a problem from one agent to another agent or to a pool of agents. Escalation occurs when one agent has completed all the work that he or she can on the problem and there is still work to be done. Many service centers refer to this as routing instead of escalation, choosing to use the term escalation for nonroutine transfers. We will use the term escalation to refer to both routine and nonroutine transfers.

Routine transfers imply predefined rules and guidelines. For routine escalation to work effectively, those guidelines and rules must be well defined, firmly in place, and constantly monitored and tuned. The overall performance of the service center is greatly impacted by how well escalation is handled. In a multitiered service center, escalation is predefined to control the transfer of problems from one tier to the next. Generally, a multitiered environment is organized so that tier 1 can handle 80 percent of the problems reported. Tier 1 is usually composed of agents who are considered generalists because they have a broad range of knowledge that spans all of the products supported by the service center. Tier 2 and 3 are typically composed of experts who have more in-depth knowledge of fewer products. Tier 1 agents generally know a little about a lot of products, while tier 2 and 3 agents know a lot about one or two products. When a tier 1 agent cannot resolve a problem, it is transferred (escalated) to a tier 2 specialist. Problems can also be transferred when an agent exceeds a predefined time limit for resolving problems, when an agent does not have authority to fix a problem, when a problem is predefined to be handled at tier 2 or 3, or when a customer asks for the problem to be escalated (nonroutine).

7.4.1 Defining Escalation

To successfully handle escalation, the service center must define

- What items can be escalated
- When those items should be escalated
- What information must be gathered prior to escalating
- Where the item is transferred (which group or person receives it)
- Service levels for escalated problems

- Ownership and responsibility of escalated items
- What must be communicated to the customer

The easiest way to define and organize this information is on a service-by-service basis. For each service, you should define whether or not the item can be escalated, under what circumstances it can be escalated, what information should be gathered prior to escalating (what the next agent will need), where the service is escalated (the agent or pool of agents), the receiving agent's responsibility, and what the sending agent should tell the customer. Some of these things will span all services or a group of services, and so do not need to be redefined for each service. For example, service levels such as expected response time by the receiving agent are most likely consistent across all products and services that the agent receives and are based more on the priority. However, if there is a unique service level for a service, it should be documented. If any special information is required by the receiving agent, you should document this for the service to ensure that the sending agent gathers that information prior to transferring the problem. This may prevent the receiving agent from having to contact the customer.

A service catalog is a helpful tool for defining escalation. For the purposes of escalation, limit the list to any service that can be escalated. Your service catalog may closely mirror your subject tree and include services such as product A support, product B support, and so forth. You can certainly subdivide each of those into lower levels if you choose to, or need to, to accommodate escalation. To decide the appropriate level, consider if tier 1 agents have authority to handle all aspects of support for the product in question or if certain aspects are escalated automatically. For example, suppose product A is Microsoft Exchange. Tier 1 agents can support many components of Exchange and can resolve a wide variety of problems. However, if a customer calls and requests a new mail box, the tier 1 agent does not have the authority to create one.

Once the service catalog is defined, you can define all the important information for each service. For each service, you should define where it is initially handled. Is tier 1 responsible for providing this service or does it go immediately to a tier 2 pool? Document the escalation path for each service. The escalation path shows the group that starts the service and then which group it moves to when escalation is required. Table 7–1 is an example of an escalation plan.

Table 7–1   Where Items Are Escalated

Product	Service	Tier 1				Tier 2		Tier 3		
		Pool A	Pool B	Pool C	Pool D	Pool E	Pool F	Pool G	Pool H	Pool I
Prod A	1	R				R		R		
	2	R			R				R	
	3	D	D	D			R		R	
	4	R				R				R
Prod B		R	R	R	R					R
Prod C	1			R	R					R
	2			R	R					R
	3			R	R					R
Prod D			R				R	R		

In Table 7–1, supported products are subdivided into services provided for that product. Service 2 of product A is received and resolved (R) by the tier 1 pool A. If they have to escalate the problem, it goes to tier 2 pool D. If tier 2 pool D can't resolve the problem, it is escalated to tier 3, pool H. Notice that you can follow the escalation path on a service-by-service basis. Notice that product A service 3 can be received by any tier 1 pool, but is immediately dispatched (D) to tier 2 pool F. If product A were Microsoft Exchange, service 3 might be Add a New Mailbox, which according to company policy must be done by tier 2 pool F. You can use any variety of methods to document this information, but a spreadsheet may be useful because you can sort by resource pool to get a complete list of services that each pool provides. The combination of product and service columns can match your subject tree. The other benefit of this approach is that you can use the table to set up the automatic escalation capabilities of your PMS (if it supports this function). Most PMSs allow you to set a time-limit trigger that automatically escalates the ticket to the predefined person or group when a certain amount of time has gone by. Many systems base escalation and routing on predefined paths based on the product or service selected for the ticket.

This may seem like a lot of work, and it is, but it is definitely worth it. You expect your agents to know what to do with problems, so you should define it or formalize it. If your agents are already routing tickets based on a general understanding of which pools handle which problems, you should get representatives from those pools together and go through this exercise. It is amazing how quickly problems surface and require clarification. It is generally an eye-opening experience for everyone involved. The other benefit is that if there are services immediately dispatched from tier 1 to tier 2, this spreadsheet can be sorted to show them to you. If you want tier 1 to handle more services, this creates your list of possible services to move to tier 1 for resolution. This too is an eye-opening experience, because tier 2 or 3 resources may be reluctant to give up responsibility for a host of reasons. If you hear comments like "The tier 1 resources don't have the skills" or "The tier 1 agents can't have the authority to do that," you should closely consider those statements to determine if tier 1 one truly can't handle the service or if tier 2 doesn't want to give up turf. You can cut and paste these tier 2 services into yet another spreadsheet and document the prerequisites for moving the service to tier 1. Those prerequisites could include training and tools that must be implemented. You could also document key milestones for each service, showing when tools must be implemented, when training must be complete, and when the cut-over is scheduled to occur.

Special Data Requirements

You can create a similar spreadsheet that captures any special data that one tier must gather before escalating the request to a subsequent tier. Why would you want to go to this trouble? Take the time to document this because it could save you time and save your customers frustration. Standard information is required for all service requests, but some types of problems will always require the same additional information. When this is the case, you should expect the tier 1 agent to gather that data before escalating the problem to the tier 2 agent. Your PMS may have the ability to add these as mandatory fields when the agent selects the category from the subject tree.

When to Escalate

Some requests may be escalated immediately, for example, when the tier 1 agents have no responsibility to resolve the problem or service the request. An example is a hardware problem. For these requests, the problem is automatically escalated to the tier 2 resource pool that handles hardware support (after the tier 1 agent gathers the basic information and any special data predefined as a requirement).

Requests can be escalated based on the customer's request to do so. You need to have rules about this. If the customer requests to speak to a manager, you should accommodate that request immediately. This means that you must predefine the managers who receive these requests for each shift.

You should be prepared to handle customers who want to be escalated to a tier 2 resolution pool because he or she does not have faith that tier 1 can handle it. Generally, you should implement a rule that says if tier 1 is the resource pool that should handle the problem, then they must take first crack at it, even if the customer doesn't want them to. If the customer doesn't like that, he or she can be escalated to a manager, who will explain the policy and then decide if and where to escalate the call.

Requests can be escalated when the agent has done all that he or she can do to resolve the problem and there is still work to be done. Some service centers place limits on the amount of time a tier 1 agent can work on a particular call. If the request is still not serviced when that time expires, the agent escalates that request to the appropriate tier 2 pool. Generally, tier 2 and tier 3 do not have time limits. Time limits are important for controlling the number of tier 1 agents required to handle call volume, but can negatively impact your tier 1 resolution rates. Establishing tier 1 time limits always creates a trade-off between tier one resolution rates and staffing levels. Finding the appropriate balance is the key.

Service Levels for Escalated Problems

Service levels will most likely be tied to priorities, but it is possible that they will be tied to specific services. Some services, as defined in the subject tree, may be related to failures of infrastructure components. It is likely that failure of infrastructure components, such as key servers, will have service levels (performance guarantees) defined. When this is the case, it is beneficial to capture that information with the service request so that the agent knows what the commitments are for that service. This also allows you to base some escalation on priority, so that a failed server is automatically routed to an emergency response team. As an example, suppose that the subject tree had WAN as the product and each link in the WAN was a separate service. You may have an SLA in place that guarantees 15-minute response for customer A when link 3 is down.

7.4.2 Typical Escalation Problems

Many service centers have low tier 1 resolution rates, which is often a result of escalating far too many problems. The primary reason for excessive escalating is a lack of training for many items that could and should be handled at tier 1; tier 1 was designed to handle a broad range of customer problems, but the agents do not have the training to cover all the products. When you examine their service escalation spreadsheet, you notice that a significant number of problems are automatically escalated to tier 2. The second reason so many items are escalated is the lack of a knowledge base. Many of the problems that come into the service center are problems that have been previously resolved for other customers, yet these calls are repeatedly escalated because the resolution is not available to the tier 1 service center agents.

Low resolution rates also occur when problems are frequently escalated prior to troubleshooting. This leads to problems being incorrectly categorized and routed to the wrong group, and too often requires additional contact with the customer. This is not just a tier 1 problem; it clearly occurs at tier 2 as well. When this happens, the wrong person troubleshoots the problem, discovers the real problem, reroutes the problem to the correct person, and often does not update the ticket to reflect that it has been rerouted. The correct person finally takes on the problem, troubleshoots it yet again, fixes it, and updates the ticket. (The customer may or may not be informed of the fix; see the section "Ticket Ownership" in this chapter).

One final note regarding escalation: One of the reasons there are problems with many service centers' escalation process is that it is often unknown who to escalate to. This is true for two reasons. Continual reorganizations can cause confusion about which groups are responsible for which parts of the infrastructure, as well as confusion about which people belong to which groups. As a result, problems are routed to the former expert, regardless of his or her current responsibilities. Sometimes this results in items being escalated from tier 1 directly to tier 3. Often, a new organization is in place on paper, but not necessarily in practice.

If you have recently reorganized, you should complete the development of the service catalog or, if it already exists, update it to reflect the changes. This catalog, particularly where it focuses on problems, will show the escalation path for all problem types, thus eliminating part of the escalation problem. You should also conduct periodic follow-up meetings with the staff to clarify the new organization structure and responsibilities. Collect feedback on issues with the new structure and focus on communications, functions, and services not adequately covered.

7.4.3 Escalation Initial Response Times

It is important to document initial response times (IRTs) by tier for escalated items. The response times will vary based on the priority of the problems being escalated. You must develop IRTs by tier in order to control the delivery times to the customer. These IRTs may or may not be documented in SLAs or service contracts.

Assume you have target resolution times for each priority level of problems, as illustrated in Table 7–2. To achieve those targets in a multitiered organization, you must control how long one tier should work on a problem until those agents pass it on to the next tier. You then must control how long that problem sits in the next tier's queue until those agents begin work. How long should the agents in tier 2 work on the problem before escalating to tier 3? For example, suppose your target resolution time for priority level 2 problems is 4 hours. Should the tier 1 agent work on the problem for 30 minutes before escalating to tier 2? How long can it sit in the tier 2 queue before a tier 2 agent picks it up and begins work? Controlling these intervals is the only way you can hope to achieve your target resolution times and stay within your SLAs.

Table 7–2 is a sample initial response time table that shows the maximum amount of time an agent should work on a problem prior to escalating the problem. The amount of time is based on the problem priority. These are maximum times and do not preclude the agent from escalating sooner, which requires some amount of judgment on the parts of the agent and management. The service center manager or shift manager should monitor these escalations to make sure that the service center agents are not escalating without first giving the issue a reasonable amount of effort.

Table 7–2 Sample Service Center Priority Level and Initial Response Times

Priority Level	Severity	Tier 1	Work Time Before Escalating*	Tier 2 Initial Response Time**	Work Time Before Escalating	Tier 3 Initial Response Time***	Target Resolution Time
1	Critical	Take Call	15 min.	15 min.	1 hour	15 min.	2 hours
2	Urgent	Take Call	30 min.	30 min.	1 hour	15 min.	4 hours
3	Important	Take Call	2 hours	2 hours	2 hours	1 hour	8 hours
4	Low	Take Call	8 hours	4 hours	8 hours	4 hours	3 days
5	Monitor	Take Call			No Escalation		

Tier 1 Work Time Before Escalating could be 0 minutes for some problems, such as hardware, which are automatically escalated to a tier 2 hardware resource pool.

**Tier 2 Initial Response Time* is the length of time between the tier 1 service center escalation to tier 2 and the tier 2 response to the request for service. In other words, this indicates the maximum time the escalated problem can sit in queue before a tier 2 agent takes ownership of the problem and begins work.

***Tier 3 Initial Response Time* is the length of time between the tier 2 service center escalation to tier 3 and the tier 3 response to the request for service. As above, it represents the maximum amount of time the problem can sit in a tier 3 queue before an agent takes ownership.

The sample table also documents IRT commitments for the tier 2 and tier 3 resource pools, based on ticket priority level. If your service center escalates to a pool of resources, as opposed to escalating to individuals within the pool, the manager of the pool must be held accountable for the IRTs. The pool manager's performance should be partially measured based on the pool's ability to meet IRTs.

There are several items to notice about Table 7–2. First, notice that a priority level 4 problem can stay in the tier 1 queue for 8 hours. This assumes that tier 1 agents have time away from the phones to work on problems. If this is not the case, then all problems that cannot be resolved in a predefined time period must be escalated after that time is up. So, if your tier 1 agents have a time limit of, say, 10 minutes per call and they have no downtime away from the phones, then all problems not resolved during the 10 minutes must be escalated.

Notice also that if tier 1 works the maximum amount of time before escalating, and tier 2 waits the maximum amount of time before pulling the ticket from their queue and then works the maximum amount of time before escalating, tier 3 is left with very little time to resolve the problem and still achieve the target resolution time. The table shows maximum time limits to ensure that, if required, tier 3 has a chance to do some work and still achieve the target resolution times, but the problem can be escalated prior to reaching the maximums.

7.4.4 Key IRT Considerations

When you are developing your IRT and priority schedule, there are several key factors you should consider. First, and perhaps foremost, are your target resolution times. Use these to work backward. You want to give the most qualified staff members as much time as possible to solve problems while minimizing redundant work between tiers. Second, consider whether all problem types of the same priority should receive the same IRT treatment. This is perhaps the more difficult question. Should you automatically escalate an issue that would normally be handled by a tier 1 agent? In other words, do you give the tier 1 agent a chance to work on a priority 1 problem, or do you escalate it immediately? Or, does it depend on the type of problem? You may have certain types of priority 1 issues that you expect a tier 1 agent to attempt to resolve, and others that you expect the agent to escalate immediately. At priority level 2, you may expect the tier 1 agent to attempt resolution on all issues, as they normally do.

It is a lot of work, but you must take the time to determine how IRTs will be handled. Work with representatives from each tier to develop the solution. Be careful not to send the wrong message to tier 1 agents, that is, that they lack the skills to handle priority 1 problems. Many service centers have emergency response teams that handle all priority 1 problems.

One final note: If you are implementing IRTs by tier for the first time or if you already have them but suspect that they are being ignored, you should track response time for every escalated ticket. Measure IRT by pool owner and use this information as a performance measure for that pool owner. This may be the only way to make the pool owners take ownership of IRT. This will force the pool owners to pay much more attention to what is being escalated to them and, in turn, will force them to communicate problems to the service center manager or to other pool owners, or to both.

7.4.5 Escalation Notifications

Most service centers maintain a notification schedule that corresponds to the IRT table. Notifications are used in conjunction with priority-based IRTs to ensure that the service center can respond appropriately to customer problems. This is particularly important in a multitier, multipool structure. Now that you have defined IRTs for each tier, based on priority and perhaps problem type, what managerial notifications should occur to oversee the process?

The notification schedule documents who should be contacted and when. The three key factors in developing the schedule are the problem priority level, the type of problem, and the time of day. The priority level is used to determine which managers, or level of management within the service center, should be notified. Should the service center manager or CIO be notified of all priority 1 problems, and if so, when and how? Should they be beeped immediately, or within 15 minutes?

The problem type determines which pool manager and resources within a pool should be notified. Is it a desktop software problem, a network problem, a hardware problem, or a telecom problem? If it is a priority 1 with a server, the manager of the telecom pool probably does not need to be notified, but the manager of the pool that handles server problems does.

The time of day, of course, determines who to contact, based on priority and problem type during the three shifts. It will also determine how to reach that person, based on time of day. Assuming a priority 1 network problem occurs at 3:00 A.M., how do you reach the appropriate pool manager? Who else is notified, and how do you reach them? SLAs may also require that you contact a customer.

The notifications table (Table 7–3) shows which manager should be notified after the passage of a predetermined amount of time for each priority level. These times are maximums. There is no reason that a particular group or resource poolcan't establish a faster response time. Table 7–3 is generic. Your table should have actual employee names, contact methods, and numbers. The table should also have a third dimension to show who to contact during each shift and on weekends, or more simply, you could have a different table for each shift. The tables should also have primary and backup contacts in case a primary cannot be reached.

Table 7–3 Escalation Notifications Table

Priority Level	T1 IRT** Warning Notification	Notify	T2 IRT*** Warning Notification	Notify	T3 IRT Warning Notification	Notify	Target Resolution Time
1	*1+0 min.	SC Manager	1+15 min.	T2 Pool Owner	1+90 min.	T3 Pool Owner	2 hours
				SC Manager		SC Manager	
			1+35 min.	T2 Pool Owner	1+120 min.	T3 Pool Owner	
				SC Manager		SC Manager	
				Escalate to Pool Owner's Manager		Escalate to Pool Owner's Manager	
2	1+15 min.	SC Manager	1+30 min.	T2 Pool Owner	1+120 min.	T3 Pool Owner	4 hours
				SC Manager		SC Manager	
			1+75 min.	T2 Pool Owner	1+165 min.	T3 Pool Owner	
				SC Manager		SC Manager	
				Escalate to Pool Owner's Manager		Escalate to Pool Owner's Manager	
3	1+60 min.	SC Manager	1+90 min.	T2 Pool Owner	1+300 min.	T3 Pool Owner	8 hours
				SC Manager		SC Manager	
			1+180 min.	T2 Pool Owner	1+420 min.	T3 Pool Owner	
				SC Manager		SC Manager	
				Escalate to Pool Owner's Manager		Escalate to Pool Owner's Manager	
4	1+2 days	SC Manager	1+3 days	T2 Pool Owner	1+12 hours	T3 Pool Owner	24 hours
				SC Manager		SC Manager	
			1+4 days	T2 Pool Owner	1+20 hours	T3 Pool Owner	
				SC Manager		SC Manager	
				Escalate to Pool Owner's Manager		Escalate to Pool Owner's Manager	

(*continued*)

Table 7–3   Escalation Notifications Table (*Continued*)

Priority Level	T1 IRT** Warning Notification	Notify	T2 IRT*** Warning Notification	Notify	T3 IRT Warning Notification	Notify	Target Resolution Time
5	1+2 days	SC Manager	1+3 days	T2 Pool Owner	1+4 days	T3 Pool Owner	5 days
				SC Manager		SC Manager	
			1+4 days	T2 Pool Owner	1+5 days	T3 Pool Owner	
				SC Manager		SC Manager	
				Escalate to Pool Owner's Manager		Escalate to Pool Owner's Manager	

*I = incident and represents the time the incident is first reported to the service center. Therefore, I + 15 min means 15 minutes after the incident is reported to the service center.

**T1 = tier 1; T2 = tier 2; T3 = tier 3.

***IRT= initial response time. For tier 1, IRT represents the time from the initial report of the incident. For tier 2, IRT represents the difference between the time the incident was escalated and when someone in a tier 2 resource pool took ownership of the ticket.

Priority Level 1: Urgent

This is the highest priority level and therefore has the shortest notification period. When a level 1 priority problem is reported to the service center, the service center manager (SC manager) and the shift manager should be notified of the problem immediately (*I* + 0 min means time incident reported plus zero minutes). This may or may not be the case for your service center, so work with the managers to determine the most appropriate schedule. The manager can then make sure the escalation and notification procedures are followed and response time commitments are achieved. He or she should also verify the priority level and bring the proper resources to bear.

Since the target resolution time for level 1 priorities is 2 hours, the tier 2 pool owner responsible for the problem must be notified as well. In this sample, the pool manager is notified if the incident is not resolved within 15 minutes of being reported. Again, this is a maximum of 15 minutes, and the pool owner could be notified sooner. In this sample, the SC manager is notified immediately, while the tier 2 pool owner is notified no more than 15 minutes later. In reality, it will probably be the other way around; that is, the tier 2 pool owner is notified immediately, and then the service center manager is notified only if the problem is not resolved within 15 minutes.

Finally, if the ticket has been escalated to a tier 2 pool and after 35 minutes the ticket is still open, the SC manager, the tier 2 pool owner, and the tier 2 pool owner's manager are all notified. Obviously, the intent is to ensure that the problem receives the attention it deserves. IT management may take action to reprioritize and shift workload so resources can be brought to bear on the problem, or they may have to meet with the affected client, or both.

Since the target resolution time for level 1 priorities is 2 hours, the appropriate tier 3 pool owner is notified if the incident is not resolved within 90 minutes of being reported. Again, this is a maximum of 90 minutes, and the manager could be notified sooner.

If after 2 hours, the ticket is still open, the next higher level of management should be notified. This includes notification to, perhaps, the vice president or CIO level of the service center or IT department.

This level of management is involved by exception, that is, when target resolution times are missed. This level of management can also be involved earlier, when it is anticipated that target resolution times will be missed. Management should reassign resources as required to address the problem and begin or pick up communications with the client.

The combination of service escalation paths, escalation IRT, and priority-level notifications are key to successfully managing the service center and getting the job done for your customers. The combination establishes where problems are handled, what resources are brought to bear, and when and who will oversee the problem to ensure that any obstacles to resolution are removed. It also allows for proactive communication with the customer. Finally, most problem management systems automate time-based notification and time-based escalation. Developing these schedules will greatly simplify the setup process for the problem management system.

7.5 Tier 1, 2, and 3 Problem Management Responsibilities

To make sure the escalation process works smoothly, the service center agents must be sure they have done their due diligence prior to escalating a problem from one tier to the next. To do this, it is very important to clearly define the responsibilities of each of the service center tiers and make sure that everyone in the service center understands those responsibilities.

For incidents that are automatically escalated from tier 1 to tier 2, such as hardware incidents, the tier 1 agents are still responsible for researching and analyzing the issue prior to escalation. This is to ensure that the incident really should be escalated. Searching the knowledge base in these cases may reveal a new solution that could be rendered at tier 1 without having to escalate. The tier 1 agents should not escalate without researching the issue first. The same holds true for tier 2 escalations to tier 3. While this sounds, and is, simplistic, many service centers escalate far too many issues without researching and troubleshooting the problem first. The lack of proper research means that too many incidents are escalated that could have and should have been handled without escalation. The lack of research also results in issues that are escalated to the wrong resource pool. This of course means that issues must be rerouted (allowing some to fall through the cracks) and that the wrong resource has spent time troubleshooting a problem.

The key objectives in multitier problem management are to

1. Make sure all agents who participate in the service center understand their service center responsibilities.
2. Make sure all agents who participate in the service center live up to those responsibilities.

The responsibilities for each of the tiers are shown in Table 7–4. The following recommendations will help ensure smooth tier management.

1. Make these responsibilities part of all service center employees' job descriptions and performance reviews.
2. Gather metrics to measure each employee's success in meeting his or her responsibilities.
3. Train the staff on these responsibilities and discuss the utilization of the responsibilities in performance reviews.

Table 7–4 Tier 1, 2, and 3 Problem Management Responsibilities

Item	Tier 1 Responsibilities	Tier 2 and Tier 3 Responsibilities
Customer Relationship	Manage "cradle to grave" relationship with customer. Keep customer informed when status changes. Inform customer what to expect. Communicate commitments such as initial response times and target resolution times. Follow up with all escalated issues. Follow up with customer within x days of closure.	Update ticket as necessary. Keep service center informed when status changes. Meet or exceed initial response times. Own the customer's problem.
Customer Validation	Verify customer information. Ensure customer is a valid customer. Verify requested service is a valid service. Verify customer eligibility to receive requested service. Enforce service center policies.	Generally, none. Tier 2 and 3 agents should not, generally, be the customer's first contact. If it does occur, then the agent must take on the same responsibilities as a tier 1 agent.
Problem Logging	Ensure accurate capture of issue/request. Ensure issue/request is properly categorized. Verify priority. Ensure customer concurrence.	Verify/update issue request category as required.
Problem Determination	Clarify the customer problem. Document steps to reproduce and verify. Thoroughly search knowledge base for similar issues. Document all analysis. Document all solutions attempted. Provide resolution to customer. Close requests that are resolved at tier 1.	Meet initial response time commitments. Review ticket. Review knowledge base search results. Clarify problem if necessary. Develop resolution strategy. Visit customer if, and only if, necessary. Document all analysis. Document all solutions attempted. Provide resolution to customer. Update ticket/close request.

(continued)

Item	Tier 1 Responsibilities	Tier 2 and Tier 3 Responsibilities
Escalation	Escalate to tier 2 if, and only if, required. Gather and document all required data prior to escalation. Ensure tier 2 agent takes ownership. Maintain responsibility for ticket. Notify customer; set expectations.	Escalate to tier 3 if, and only if, required. Gather and document all required data prior to escalation.
Knowledge Base	Create new knowledge base reports as required. Ensure quality of new knowledge base reports. Update existing knowledge base reports as required. Ensure quality of updates to existing reports.	Create new knowledge base reports as required. Ensure quality of new knowledge base reports. Update existing knowledge base reports as required. Ensure quality of updates to existing reports.

Note: Tier 3 responsibilities are the same as tier 2, except there may be no escalation.

▶ 7.6 Service Request (Ticket) Ownership

Service request ownership is a serious responsibility, the key objectives of which are to

1. Never let a customer slip through the cracks.
2. Never make a customer someone else's responsibility.
3. Manage the customer from cradle to grave.
4. Inspire confidence from the customer.
5. Delight the customer.

In most service centers, ticket ownership transfers with the ticket when the ticket is escalated. Unfortunately, this can lead to customer dissatisfaction, because in many cases, no one ends up with responsibility for the customer. If and when customers call back to the service center for status updates, it is obvious to the customer that no one has much of an idea of their status. In many service centers, tier 2 and tier 3 agents do *not* take responsibility, or consistently take responsibility, for the ticket itself. They may do a fine job of restoring service to the client or escalating the problem, but a terrible job of updating the ticket. Unfortunately, the help desk is left in a position where they are not able to answer customer questions. Often, when a ticket is escalated, it just seems to disappear. Tracking control and commitments are lost.

Ownership of a ticket will transfer when a ticket is escalated to the agent receiving the ticket. This means that the agent must accept ownership for solving the customer problem. However, responsibility for the ticket and the customer should stay with the tier 1 service center agent who started the ticket or with the entire tier 1 team. Tier 1, whether it is the entire tier 1 team or the original agent, should be responsible for informing the customer of when he or she will hear from a tier 2 agent (making a commitment on the initial response time of tier 2). The agent should also inform the customer of which group will be receiving the escalated ticket. If the ticket is escalated to tier 3, the tier 1 representative who started the ticket should notify the customer of the escalation and the initial response time of a tier 3 agent. Even if the tier 2 agent informs the customer of the escalation to tier 3, the tier 1 representative should inform the customer that he or she (the representative) is aware of the progress and essentially reassure the customer by demonstrating that the issue is under control. The tier 1 representative should communicate all time commitments to the customer.

This approach will lead customers to contacting the help desk for updates instead of calling the agents or IT management. For this approach to work, the tier 2 and tier 3 staff must be very diligent in keeping the help desk informed of the status of escalated tickets. The tier 1 representatives must be much more diligent in terms of taking responsibility for the customer, even after problems have been escalated. The tier 1 representative is responsible for the customer's problem from cradle to grave.

7.6.1 Implementation of Ticket Ownership

It is important to note that, for several reasons, it may be more difficult to implement tier 1 ownership than it sounds. In many service centers, it requires a complete change of attitude for all tiers of the staff, but particularly for the tier 1 staff. Second, it requires that the tier 1 agents spend more time on each ticket. This could include many follow-up calls to tier 2 and tier 3 staff for awhile, until those tiers do a better job of updating tickets in a timely fashion. In addition, the tier 1 staff should proactively inform customers of problem status and must follow up with every customer to make sure that they are satisfied.

To accomplish this strategy, you may have to consider adding additional tier 1 staff. The problem management team should closely monitor and review this process. It may be necessary to force the tier 2 and tier 3 staff to update tickets in a timely fashion, and you may have to provide them with tools to accomplish this. It will also be critical to measure the amount of additional time this requires for the tier 1 staff and continue to reevaluate and adjust the tier 1 staffing requirements.

A variation of this approach is to have the entire tier 1 staff, as a team, take responsibility for follow-up with the customer as well as with tier 2 and tier 3 staff. Tier 1 agents would share responsibility for following up on escalations and with clients. The biggest risk with this approach is a lack of commitment by the individuals who comprise the team. It may be necessary to start by making each individual responsible, and then later, after changing the culture and instilling the sense of ownership, switching to team ownership.

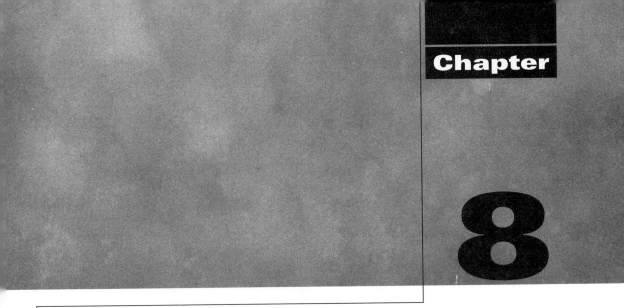

Knowledge Capture and Sharing

The knowledge capture and sharing process, or simply the knowledge capture process, is critical to the success of the service center (see Figure 8–1). This process documents and distributes the service center's institutional knowledge. In some companies, the most successful agents aren't necessarily the most technically knowledgeable; they are those best at finding information in the knowledge base. Every problem, once identified, should be evaluated as a candidate to be documented in the knowledge base. The knowledge base should be the first step in the agent's troubleshooting process.

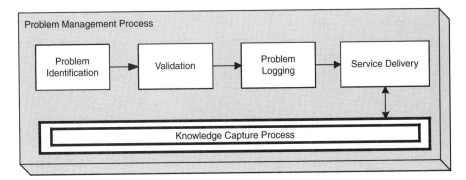

Figure 8–1   The knowledge is critical to the success of a service center.

The key objectives in knowledge capture and sharing are to

1. Create a knowledge base report for every recurring problem.
2. Make sure that each knowledge base report documents one, and only one, problem. Each problem may have many related symptoms, many workarounds, and one or more permanent resolutions.
3. Ensure the quality of the data captured in the knowledge base via a review and approval process prior to releasing information into the knowledge base.

▶ 8.1 Knowledge Capture and Sharing Overview

Many organizations do not have a knowledge base or they have one that is not used. This of course leads to redundant and unnecessary troubleshooting of the same problems nearly every time they occur. Further, it leads to different and potentially inconsistent solutions being provided for the same problem. Finally, because there is no knowledge base of problems, there are no metrics indicating how often the same problem occurs, and therefore no root cause analysis. This leads to continued occurrence of the problem and, potentially, treatment of only the symptoms, not the real problem.

The knowledge base serves many purposes. Key among these is to speed up delivery of services—problem resolution, in this case—to the customer base. This is possible because once discovered, all problems and their resolutions or workarounds, or both, are captured in the knowledge base. This allows the tier 1 service center personnel to provide an immediate resolution to many problems during the initial phone call, even problems that would normally go beyond their skill level.

Another purpose of the knowledge base is to provide consistent and accurate resolution information to the customer base. This is possible with a knowledge base because the same solution or workaround will be provided to the same problem each time that the service center personnel access the knowledge base report. If better workarounds or solutions become available, the knowledge base communicates that information to all agents.

Table 8–1 provides an example template to use for the knowledge base report. Each knowledge base report *must* describe one, and only one, problem or issue. This is important for two reasons. First, this simplifies searching and retrieving data from the knowledge base. All descriptions and resolutions are tied to one knowledge base report. When that report is found, no more searching is required. This also makes it easier to organize, and therefore search, the knowledge base.

The second reason it is important to limit each knowledge base report to a single issue is that it allows for the creation of better metrics. For example, it is possible to track the number of times the report was used and therefore the number of times that the incident occurred. You can add a field to your problem ticket to indicate which knowledge base report was used to resolve the problem. As an alternative, you can add each applicable ticket number to the knowledge base report or keep a cross reference table. Keeping track of the relationship between reported problems and knowledge base reports can result in valuable information. If a better workaround or a permanent solution becomes available, you can use the cross-reference to proactively push the information to previously impacted customers. This approach may not be feasible for large service centers, because the cross-reference can quickly become extremely large and unmanageable.

Table 8–1   Knowledge Base Report Information

Title or Tag Line of Problem (for example, cannot insert picture as float over text)		
Product Applicability	Product	List the products that this report applies to.
	Version	List each product version impacted.
	Environment	List the environments where the problem occurs (for the given product/version combo).
Problem Description	Symptoms	Describe the symptoms. (This should be a more detailed description of the title/tag line.)
	Detailed Description	If necessary, add details for each symptom.

(continued)

Table 8–1   Knowledge Base Report Information (*Continued*)

Title or Tag Line of Problem (for example, cannot insert picture as float over text)		
	Instructions to Reproduce	If necessary, add detailed description to re-create the problem step-by-step for each product/symptom affected.
Other Notes		
Cause	Document the cause of the problem, if known and if applicable.	
Status	If the cause is a bug or future enhancement, document the status of repair or enhancement.	
Solution	If there are solutions, describe each in detail. If a download or patch is available, reference it here and, if possible, provide access so the agent can give it to the customer.	
Workaround	If there is no solution, describe the workarounds available. Describe each workaround separately. There may be different workarounds for each product/version/environment.	
Report Information	Category	
	Creator/Owner	
	Date/Time Created	
	Last Revised Date	
	Reviewed by	
	Approved by	
Change Request Tracking Information	Either Notes or a Reference Number	
	Change Request Status	

▶ 8.2 Knowledge Capture Process

The knowledge capture process has four subprocesses, shown in Figure 8–2. They are initiation, knowledge capture, review and approval, and release. The knowledge capture process is most often initiated from within the problem management process. It is initiated when a previously undocumented problem or symptom is encountered during the support delivery process. The process is also initiated when the internal testing or quality assurance (QA) group identify problems. These groups can initiate the process before something developed internally is released into the customer environment or when something new is discovered after release into the environment. In either case, the process should be initiated so the information can be captured. The process should also be initiated when a change request has been completed or when a defect has been repaired. This ensures that changes and repairs are available to agents and customers. If other groups within IT are responsible for distributing (software) or making the changes (server upgrade, etc.), the knowledge base should be updated prior to distribution so that agents have access to the latest information. The update to the knowledge report can be as simple as updating the change request field to indicate that the work is done, but it will most likely be more involved. For example, the new documentation may include a link to the new code so that it can be downloaded and an updated solution that provides detailed installation instructions.

The knowledge capture process is also initiated when you purchase new knowledge base content or when a vendor product you support releases a new list of known bugs. The new information must be incorporated into your knowledge base environment. How the information is incorporated depends on your knowledge base, the way you create and store knowledge base reports, and the format and volume of the new knowledge base content. As shown in Figure 8–2, the data can be integrated into an existing knowledge base or kept as standalone. The process of making the new data available varies from service center to service center and product to product, and so is not covered in any detail.

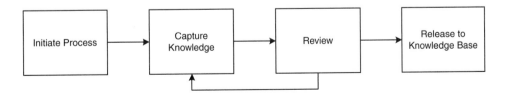

Figure 8–2   Four subprocesses of the knowledge capture process.

Once the process has been initiated, the next step is to capture the new knowledge. When an undocumented problem is discovered, the agent must create the knowledge base report, or it must be assigned to an another agent for development. If a new symptom is found, or the existing symptoms require update, the agent makes the updates. The agent may be adding a new solution, an alternate solution, or eliminating other interim solutions by putting in the final resolution. If the agent discovers more than one solution, he or she should describe and update each resolution until all resolutions are documented. While only one of multiple solutions may be the preferred solution (which should be indicated), they should all be documented so that if one fails to work for the customer, the others can be tried. Again, this allows for the quick delivery of consistent solutions to the customer base. If a solution is not currently available, then the report should reflect what is being done. This may mean that a change request was initiated or a defect was reported. It is important to document this information so that the service center staff can tell the customer that a resolution does not exist, but that someone is working on the problem. It also ensures that multiple change requests and defect reports are not initiated for the same problem. These steps will prevent the problem from being unnecessarily escalated and additional time being spent troubleshooting the problem.

Some service centers limit the knowledge base reports that are available to customers. In this scenario, service center agents have access to all reports and only a subset is available to customers. This makes sense if there are solutions or actions documented in knowledge base reports that are not applicable to customers. For example, suppose a knowledge report exists to address a recurring problem on a particular server. To execute the solution, the agent must have administration rights. There is no need to allow customers to view this report. In fact, tier 1 agents may not need to review the report. If they don't need to review it, it is best to remove it from their domain of retrievable reports so that their searches are faster and they can find solutions more quickly. In some centers, this separation is implemented as separate knowledge bases. The agent creating or modifying the report should specify the user domains that have access to the report or determine which knowledge base(s) will contain the report.

Once the agent creates or updates the report, the report does *not* go directly into the knowledge base. The content of the knowledge base report must be reviewed for both quality and accuracy. The quality review must focus on format and wording. The report must be reviewed to make sure that it follows the standard format. A standard format makes the reports easier to use and easier to write. The wording should be as clear and as concise as possible. Does the report accurately describe the symptoms, the problem, and the resolution(s)? Do the descriptions make sense, and will others, such as tier 1 service center personnel and customers, be able to understand them? This is particularly important if you plan to give your customers direct access to the knowledge base. If the report fails either of these checks, then it should be sent back to the agent who wrote it, to a more experienced agent, or to a tech writer. If your service center adds or updates very many reports, you will probably need a tech writer. Many agents are great technicians but poor writers. A good tech writer can convert an agent's gibberish into reports that customers and other less-technical agents and can actually use.

The knowledge base report must also be reviewed for technical accuracy. It would be potentially disastrous, at least embarrassing, if a bad solution was documented in the knowledge base and then propagated out to the customer base. The amount of testing performed is a function of the capabilities of your testing lab and your testing culture. In general, the more testing the better.

After the format, quality, and technical reviews have been completed, a final overall quality scan should be performed to make sure there is no extraneous information in the report, that the report is one you will not be embarrassed to put in front of your customer, and that the report is destined to be used by the correct group and released into the correct knowledge base. The final scan should be completed by the person who has final approval authority to release reports into the knowledge base.

The detailed knowledge capture process is shown in Figure 8–3.

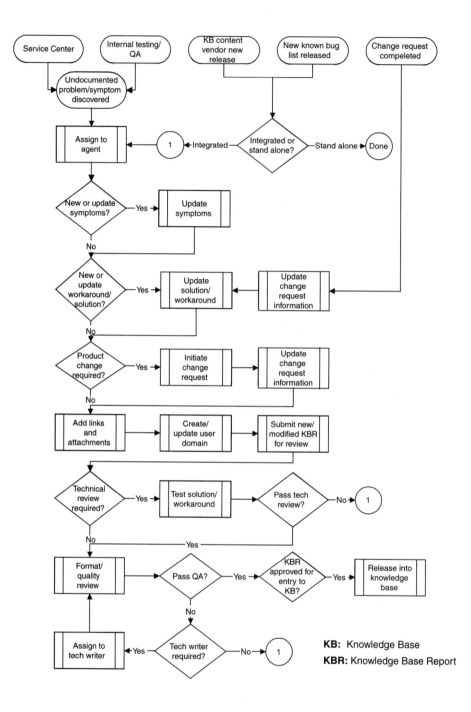

Figure 8–3 Knowledge capture process.

134

▶ 8.3 Implementation

Once you have decided what type of knowledge base to implement (see Chapter 11, "Service Center Tools") you must determine other important implementation information. You must decide who will have access, how to provide that access, how to organize the reports, how and when to remove reports (delete or archive), how often to update indexes, how to handle disaster recovery, and so on. Once these standard system implementation issues have been addressed, there are several knowledge base-specific issues you need to address. How will you populate the knowledge base? Does it come with content? Are there existing reports to be added initially? You should consider dedicating a knowledge base czar for some initial period of time. The czar may or may not be the implementation manager, but must function as the content manager. If you are implementing the first knowledge base in your data center, you will absolutely need the czar. The czar must determine

- If content should be purchased and if so, from which provider.
- The format of the reports created in-house.
- How the backlog of institutional knowledge will be captured.
- The access domains to be used for granting access to the reports.
- The access rights for each access domain (read/write/update/delete).
- The number of tech writers required (if any).
- Who will be responsible for technical reviews.
- Who will be responsible for quality reviews.

The czar must also work with managers outside of the service center. It is important to work with the manager of software development, for example, to ensure that the software development group creates reports or at least initiates the knowledge capture process when defects are repaired. The czar must take part in the change management process to ensure that knowledge reports are created and updated when applicable change requests are initiated or completed.

The czar must also take ownership of training and usage. While the process of creating and using knowledge base reports is new, someone needs to play the role of expert and champion. Creating knowledge base reports is not easy, and most technicians will resist creating them when they haven't had to create them before. This means that a champion has to be available to provide encouragement. Further, until everyone who uses the processes, both internal and external, becomes intimately familiar with them, an expert is required. The czar must play the expert role for some time.

Every recurring problem that is not documented in the knowledge base should initiate the knowledge base process. This will be a challenge initially, because nearly every problem reported to the service center will be a new problem. While this is not a trivial amount of work, it is the best way to share information and will improve the performance of the service center. Service center employees will always be armed with the latest information and will not waste time addressing issues that have already been resolved or are being worked. The czar will have to help the staff determine which problems should generate new reports.

The position of knowledge base czar should only be considered a short term-job. It should take 6 months or less to establish and tune the knowledge capture and sharingprocess. After that time, everyone involved should be familiar enough with the processes that the czar will no longer be required as a dedicated expert. Further, the capture and usage of knowledge base information should be firmly institutionalized by then, so that a champion will no longer be required. The merits of the system will act as the champion. The administrative and management responsibilities for the knowledge base should be significantly less after 6 months, so the remaining responsibilities can be transferred elsewhere within the organization.

One final note: Consider communicating changes to the knowledge base to the entire service center staff. This can be accomplished by creating an index of weekly changes (include the name of the knowledge base report and the short description) and publishing that list in a public folder called, for instance, Knowledge Base. It would be extremely user friendly if each of the indexes were hot links to the actual knowledge base report (similar to Internet query results), which would allow agents to quickly scan the titles of the new reports and hot link to those they are interested in.

Management, Review, and Oversight

There are three key components to management review and oversight of the problem management function: a plan with measurable objectives, metrics, and formal review of those metrics. We can think of these as the strategic, tactical, and operational level tasks of the problem management function. First, you must establish problem management objectives. This is your strategic task. You must then determine which metrics to gather to monitor your progress toward achieving those objectives. You must also meet with your key team leaders to review those metrics. These are your tactical tasks. Finally, you must conduct operational level meetings with your team leaders to review operational level information, such as ticket exceptions, and take corrective action when necessary.

Metrics are the key to your success. Knowing where you are and where you are going can only be established through metrics. You can communicate what you have accomplished and what you will accomplish only by the use of metrics. The only way you can expect to manage the performance of your organization is by checking performance metrics and making course adjustments as necessary. Metrics are also absolutely critical in establishing good morale within your organization and keeping your teams motivated.

▶ 9.1 Building Your Plan: Strategic Objectives and Metrics

As the manager of the problem management function, or some component of the problem management function, creating a plan is one of your most important functions. Choose objectives carefully and wisely, because this is how you will measure your performance, and may be how your manager reviews your performance. Even if your organization doesn't formally practice management by objective (MBO), it is how most organizations think.

As a manager, your objectives are your drivers and will determine where you focus your efforts. So where do they come from? Your highest level objectives, or strategic objectives, should come from three different sources: your customers, your management, and your peers. By peers, I mean service center managers at other companies.

Your customers will obviously have needs and desires that will help you establish objectives for your service center. Customers may need or demand faster initial response (less time in the queue) if you use an automated call distribution (ACD) system and they are forced to wait for the next available agent. They may need service at times when you don't normally have staff available. As you are well aware, your customers have many such needs and desires. Once you know what those are, you can begin to create measurable objectives toward achieving them.

Your management will also help you determine your primary objectives. Depending on the type of service center you run, your management may be interested in things such as the number of leads you forward to the sales organization, the amount of incremental sales you generate, customer satisfaction levels, your service center's average cost per call compared to that of other service centers, the total costs of service, and other information. If management wants more or less in any of these areas, you have a new objective, which you can measure and then manage.

Your peers at other service centers can help you determine objectives. There are thousands of service centers out there being driven by their management and customers. They are probably doing things that you, your customers, and your management never considered. Take advantage of the cumulative knowledge of your peers by networking with your peers through the various service center networking organizations.

After working with your customers, management, and peers, you should be able to develop a complete set of high-level, long-term and short-term objectives, which form the basis of your management plan. Prioritize your objectives and review the priorities with management and customers. Again, make sure your objectives are measurable and time-bound. Now, you must figure out how to accomplish these objectives. For each objective, you need to develop a strategy and sub-objectives. Essentially, you are building a hierarchy of objectives, strategies, related projects, and sub-objectives to complete each of your high-level objectives. At this point, you are still planning and trying to establish alternatives to accomplish the priorities.

As an example, let's assume that one of your high-level objectives is to provide support over the weekend, which is something that you normally do not do. In fact, let's be specific and say that you want your clients to have immediate access to support during all nonstandard business hours, and you want to make that new service available by June 15. How are you going to do that? By developing effective strategies, which will lead to additional supporting objectives. Of the plethora of strategies available to do this, let's assume you choose three.

1. Roll the phones over to the 24/7 data center group after normal business hours.
2. Provide a cell phone, pager, and laptop on a rotating basis to employees in your tier 2 support group.
3. Implement your knowledge base (as read-only, of course) on your intranet or the Internet and make it available to your entire customer base.

Each of these three strategies has measurable and time-bound objectives associated with it. The time is bound by the high-level objective, which is June 15 in this case, and may be sooner. Each strategy may require one or more projects to implement it. To accomplish the first strategy, you may have to set up the phones for automatic rollover, create and negotiate a service level agreement (SLA) with the data center, purchase and implement additional seats for your help desk tool, and provide training to the data center team. Each of these tasks will have a time and a price. You may also need to develop strategies for your supporting objectives, sub-objectives, and so on. At some point in this process, you will have fleshed out a plan, a hierarchy of objectives, strategies, and supporting projects to accomplish a high-level objective.

Now you can price it, share it with your management, show them alternatives, and let them have the final decisions on how they want you to proceed and what they will allow you to spend. A well thought-out plan is an excellent method for illustrating the impact of not spending dollars on certain projects. This approach will also establish appropriate expectations for your management team. When the budgeting process is complete, you know where to focus your efforts for the next fiscal year.

▶ 9.2 Using Metrics to Measure Your Progress

Suppose you used the approach outlined above, that is, a hierarchy of objectives and strategies to build your plan. The problem management function must compete with other business functions and business units for finite capital and operations and maintenance (O&M) dollars. When you request capital dollars for a new project or request an increase in your O&M budget, you generally have to explain why the organization should invest the money in your project, rather than elsewhere in the company. Your plan shows very clearly the benefits you are attempting to achieve. Those benefits are usually expressed in terms of increased revenue, decreased costs, or improved service levels, which are all measurable objectives.

That is one of the reasons your objectives must be measurable and time bound. Suppose you received all of the requested capital and O&M for one of your high-level objectives and you have begun to implement the supporting strategies. If you can't measure your progress toward the objective, then that objective is meaningless because you have no way of knowing whether you need to take corrective action or not. The point is that when you state an objective, make sure you express it in such a way that very precisely defines what you want to achieve and over what time period. For example, you may have an objective to reduce the average price per call by $5 by December 31. You can measure and show your progress toward achieving that objective.

9.2.1 Gathering Metrics

Let's assume that at this point you have an approved and funded plan with objectives you can measure. You now need some way to gather those measurements, and you may need some baseline data to measure against. While an objective such as reducing the average price per call is measurable, it is useless if you do not have a vehicle for measuring it. If you have no way of tracking your costs per call, then you have no way of knowing whether you need to take corrective action. How do you know that your plan is working? You must determine your methodology—in this case, of calculating your cost per call—the data you need to do that, and the approach you will use to gather that data. I highly recommend that as you develop your objectives, you also establish and document the criteria you will use for measuring the objective and the methods you will use for calculating the measures.

Fortunately, most of the off-the-shelf software used in the problem management arena has the capability to track many of these metrics; in fact, it can track more data than you may need. When this is the case, good objectives will allow you to filter the plethora of data available into meaningful information. If you don't have any software or you're using homegrown software, then you have to develop this capability on your own. Even if you have the latest and greatest software, you may have to pull together data from multiple systems to get the metrics you're after. For the cost per call example, you may need data from your corporate accounting system, your help desk application, your ACD system, and from an outsourced hardware support group. The data needed will vary, depending on the methodology you choose for determining your cost per call.

9.2.2 Baseline Data

The example objective of reducing the price per call—as well as many other objectives—is based on the assumption that you have baseline data available. To know if you have reduced your average price per call by $5, you have to know your current average price per call. If you have the baseline data available, the objective would be better stated as "Reduce the average cost per call to $49 by December 31." If you do not have baseline data, then you must create it. If you do not know your current cost per call, it will be very difficult to establish a measurable objective. If you don't know where you're at, how can you set a target for where you want to be?

Don't be overly concerned if you do not have baseline data—you can get it. Use the approach outlined in the beginning of this chapter to work with management, clients, and peers to find out what is important to them and use that information to frame your objectives. You can frame an objective about your average price per call and leave the target amount blank for now. Again, as outlined above, identify the data and methodology you will use to calculate your average cost per call. Create a list of the data you need for all of your objectives, and then find out what data you have and what data is missing. For the data that is missing, try to create reasonable estimates to use for now and implement a plan for gathering the data as you move forward. Make sure you keep track of what is real data versus what are estimates and assumptions. In cases where you are using estimates, make sure you gather the real data as soon as possible. You should gather at least 6 months' worth of data to use as your baseline before you put actual numbers into your objectives. A year would be better. If you have to move forward with objectives before you have at least 6 months' of baseline data, then make sure you document and explain your assumptions and estimates. Compare your estimates to the actuals as you move forward, but do not be too hasty in changing your estimates until you have several months' worth of data. You could also attempt to gather the baseline data by reviewing 6 to 12 months worth of historical data. If it works, the result is actual baseline data to work with. The problems are that this can be an expensive, time-consuming, and daunting task, with potentially inadequate data as a result. If you are going to do this, you should develop your plan first so that you know what baseline data to gather during the project and what calculations to use to develop the baseline data.

9.2.3 Target Data

The best place to get your target data is from your peers. Many organizations gather data and publish it as benchmark data. The benchmarks will show the average and best performance for each of the benchmarked data items. If the average cost per call among the benchmarked companies is $49 and you are currently at $109, you can easily frame a new objective. If you are going to use benchmarks, make sure you are comparing apples to apples. Review the data and methodology being used to create the benchmark. As an example, if you are using the fully loaded cost (salary, benefits, share of rent, and other overhead) of each employee as one item in your average cost per call and the benchmark data uses only employee salary, then all other things being equal, your average cost per call will be higher. Also consider that even if you are using the exact data and methodology for measuring key data, the benchmark data still may not be applicable to you. For example, because of the nature of your business, you may want or need to provide a higher level of service than your peers provide in certain benchmark areas, thereby making your costs acceptably higher. Finally, carefully consider the companies that you benchmark against. Consider the industry, whether customers supported are internal, external, or both, the importance and level of service to be provided, and size. As far as size, there are certain economies of scale to consider, so it is probably best to benchmark against a company that has a similar number of customers to support and a similar ratio of customers to support staff.

When you clearly define your objectives in measurable terms, you make it easier for others to measure your success or failure in achieving those objectives. Many managers find that exposure intimidating. Therefore, choose your objectives wisely and carefully, and resist the urge to overstate what can be accomplished. This is more easily said than done when you are using objectives to compete for finite dollars during the budgeting process. Be sure to document and explain all of your assumptions.

Creating measurable objectives can be a daunting task because it is a significant amount of work, particularly the first time. Stating an objective does nothing for achieving it. For an objective such as reducing the price per call, you will obviously have one or more supporting strategies and/or supporting objectives in place to achieve the higher level objective. You must define in detail all of those strategies and objectives, and you must determine the data you will need to measure your objective and how you will gather that data. You must keep track of the hierarchy of objectives so that you know which of your objectives are at risk when one or more supporting objectives and strategies are not being met.

9.2.4 Measuring Customer Satisfaction

Customer satisfaction can be difficult to measure. Do you even need to measure it? In many cases, you have a pretty good idea if your customers are satisfied or not, particularly on small help desks where you know most of your customers. You may work for a company for which customer satisfaction isn't a top priority. This is often true for companies whose business model is to be the low-cost provider of products or services. Or, you may work for a company that just doesn't see the value (yet) of investing in providing support services.

For other companies, outstanding service is the absolute goal. In these companies, it may be that service is the key discriminator in their market place or is a critical component of their business model.

The bottom line is that even if your company places low priority on customer satisfaction, you should always attempt to measure and document your customers' level of satisfaction. The extent of the measure and the effort and cost expended should vary by the type of business your company is engaged in and by the philosophy and culture of the company's management. You are far better off to have metrics showing customers' level of satisfaction and not need them than to need those metrics and not have them. Let's say, for example, that your customers receive minimal levels of support by design and that they are not thrilled with that, but management is not willing to fork over the bucks to provide better service. At some point, one loud, squeaky wheel or many small squeaky wheels will get you invited to a meeting with the boss to explain why you are doing such a bad job. You would be far better off to go into that meeting prepared with facts showing that the service center was designed to provide minimal service rather than to attend that meeting empty-handed. In fact, if you were to go in with metrics that show where customers are most dissatisfied and a list of improvement projects to address those issues, along with the costs and a tactful reminder that the budget for those improvements was not approved, you may just survive. You may even receive approval to move forward on an improvement project. It is nearly a universal fact that management will forget that they cut those proposed projects out of your budget, and your customers won't know that you ever proposed improvements in the first place. Be prepared.

Customer satisfaction metrics are even more critical if your company's goal is to be a top-notch service provider. You must know where cus-

Chapter **9** I Management, Review, and Oversight

tomers would like to see improvement, so that you can plan and execute those improvements.

So how do you gather the elusive customer satisfaction data, what data do you gather, and how often? There are many different methods for gathering the data, but in general, you are usually after the same data. You want to know the customers' overall impression of the service they receive. Is it worth the cost you distribute or charge back to them? Do they feel they are getting value for their money? In other words, you need to understand their satisfaction with the key components of their experience. The key components of the transaction are contact, communication, understanding, thoroughness of contact or problem resolution, speed of resolution, and level of concern shown for them. During a transaction with the service center, all of those components are important to the customer. If you do all but one well, the customer will be dissatisfied. Accomplish all of them well, and the customer will be delighted.

In your customer surveys, be sure to ask how the customer feels about each component of the transaction, and why. This is where the survey gets tricky, because you are asking for a lot of information and you also want the customer to back it up with examples. Let's face it—if the customer doesn't tell you why he or she is dissatisfied, it may be very difficult to take corrective action. An obvious problem with surveys is lack of response. Response levels are low in general, but when you send a long survey and ask the customer to spend a lot of time trying to remember and document specific details, response is even lower. You have probably had the experience, as I have, of starting to fill out a survey, only to pitch it after half an hour and several pages, when you find you are just nearing the halfway point.

Keep your surveys short and focused on a particular topic. To do this probably means that you will have to send out more surveys to cover all topics, but your response rate should be higher and the feedback you receive should be better. Generally, I will spend up to 15 minutes on a survey, whether that survey has 100 questions or only 10. That means you get better data from me on the short survey than on the long one.

Certainly, the way you frame your questions is just as important as any other factor in getting back the data you require. Yes or no questions give you very good metrics to work from and they are easy for the customer to answer. Statements followed by checkboxes that indicate satisfaction are excellent as well, but they will not tell you why, for example, 15 percent of the respondents are "less than satisfied" with their initial contact. Too many questions, even simple questions, can be annoying, and perhaps people are becoming even less tolerant due to the prolific use of questionnaires on the Internet. Have you noticed how many free services are available on the Internet simply for filling out a "simple" 82-page survey? I've gotten to the point where I'll go to a different site that has a shorter questionnaire, rather than fill out a long one. I am developing an aversion to questionnaires, and your customers may be as well, especially when generic data are requested.

If the customer feels that you are requesting information that you should already have, forget about getting a response. Nothing is more annoying to me than having to type in my name on a questionnaire that was sent to me in the first place, or having to tell a vendor what equipment I have on my desktop when the vendor is the one who supplied it. In the long run, it is far better to expend the effort to gather documented information from available sources than to ask your customer to supply it again.

If you are going to send out a questionnaire, keep it as short and focused as possible, with well-framed questions. You can also add questions or checkboxes, asking if the questionnaire was difficult and whether you are sending too many or sending them too often. I have never seen those questions on a questionnaire, and would appreciate the opportunity to give such feedback. In general, people understand the importance of information and want to give feedback that contributes to improving the services they receive. Use their feedback to help you improve your survey process, as well.

The frequency of surveys is an important factor to consider. You don't want to send them so often that customers get tired of seeing them, but you must send them often enough to keep track of your performance and to get fresh data. If you send a survey once a year, you are going to get sweeping generalizations or overall impressions, at best. If you are after overall impressions, then once a year may be fine. If you want to know specifically about performance of the contact process, then you need the information more frequently.

Let's suppose that you want feedback from your customers in the following areas:

- Overall impression of the service they receive
- Specific contact information
- Communication and understanding
- Thoroughness of contact or problem resolution
- Speed of resolution
- Level of concern shown for the customer
- Quality and reliability of their (the customers') environment

If you have 10 questions (5 would be better) in each of those areas, then you have a total of 70 questions that you would like to have answered fairly frequently. It would be nice to have this feedback monthly as part of your overall monthly performance reviews. This would allow you to correlate changes in customer satisfaction with your monthly service center metrics. However, you cannot realistically expect a very high completion rate if you send the same people 70 questions a month. Instead, you can send all 70 questions out each month to different customers, rotating through your customer base, say, twice a year. You will get feedback on a monthly basis, but how it correlates to the service center's performance the month it was sent is questionable because the customers filling it out are responding only twice a year, giving you general impressions. Also, there is still the problem that you are sending out a huge questionnaire, which means response rate will be low. This is still a better approach than sending out the questionnaire to the entire customer base every 6 months, because at least you're getting feedback on a monthly basis, and from that, you can compile a 6-month rolling trend.

A better approach may be to divide your questionnaire into key areas (like the seven above) and divide your customer base into the same number of areas. Each month, send one key area survey to each of the segments of the customer base, rotating the survey sent to each customer segment on a month-by-month basis. In this scenario, the individual customer will receive a short, 10-question survey each month, which varies by key area from month to month. If you send a different key area survey to each of the customer segments, you will get feedback across all of the key areas each month. While you are much more likely to get better feedback from each customer in this scenario, you need to take the pulse of your customers to make sure that 10 questions a month is not too much. Using this approach will probably give you better feedback from customers because the surveys are short and require no more than 10 to 15 minutes of their time each month. The downside is that each customer is giving you feedback to a particular key area only once every seven months. This approach also requires more management on your part to make sure the customers are getting the correct survey each period.

Having customer feedback on a monthly basis is critical to running a successful service center. For example, if customer satisfaction with the initial contact dropped last month, then you know you need to examine your service center metrics to identify possible causes and potential solutions. You could find that the customers' wait time in the call queue increased by x seconds last month because the volume of calls increased by y percent last month. You may further identify that call volumes are increasing steadily and can then, perhaps, correlate that customer satisfaction will continue to decline unless you take some corrective action to reduce the call volume or increase the number of resources fielding those calls. There are two important points to consider here. First, you do not have to have the customer satisfaction data to identify the trend in call-wait times. If you don't have the data, though, then how do you know the impact to the customer? How do you know how much of a wait is too much, and how do you know what type of corrective action is called for? Second, consider the value of having the customer satisfaction metrics on a monthly basis versus quarterly or even less frequently. The more frequently you measure, the more proactive you can be in keeping your customers satisfied. You can take corrective action now rather than wait 6 months to find that your customers are abandoning you. You also have very compelling trend data to show your management in supporting your budget and budget requests.

Depending on how you gather customer feedback data and how frequently, it can be difficult to correlate directly to other service center metrics and specific service center problems. For example, a customer may fill out a survey he receives today and indicate that he is not satisfied with the initial contact. However, the incident he is referring to happened 6 months ago. This does not mean you can't work with the data—it just means that your data don't correlate directly. The best customer feedback you can get is feedback tied to the specific incident. If you can get feedback after each incident, it will correlate directly and really allow you to troubleshoot problems in the service center. If you collect this type of information, you probably will not have to send out any other surveys, at least not surveys that evaluate your performance.

This approach is really only feasible via email, or maybe by fax. During your call close-out process, send your customer a survey. Keep it short, focused, and simple, and prepopulate it with all the vital information, such as the incident and call ID, date and time opened and closed, a summary of the events, follow-up information, and so on. Use checkboxes and yes or no questions as much as possible. Allow space for comments, but don't require them. One of the best approaches I have seen is an email that provides the vital information, and then has three "emoticon" buttons at the bottom—a frown, a straight mouth, and a smiley face. The customer just has to press one button and an email with the result is sent back to the service center, representing the customer's overall impression of the incident. It can't be any easier.

This data can be directly correlated back to other service center metrics. You may find that 92 percent of customers who deal with service center agent 2 return a smiley face, while 85 percent of customers who deal with agent 5 return a frown. Think of what you can do with that type of data. You can reward agent 2 and monitor agent 5. It may be that agent 5 needs additional technical or interpersonal training. You can also find troublesome clients. For example, you may find that no matter which agent handles client Bob, he always returns a frown. Perhaps customer Bob needs his expectations realigned, or has a language barrier, or needs to take the Introduction to PCs course you offer. You can correlate these findings back to your subject tree also. Imagine what planning you could do if you knew that 72 percent of the incidents dealing with a particular brand of palm computing device ended with a frown from clients. Do you need more training for technicians, or is it just not the right product for your environment? How do your clients like the service they are receiving from your outsourced hardware support vendor? Does that meet with the SLA? Why is it that 84 percent of the calls that are routed/escalated to network operations result in a frown? Are network operations personnel not meeting their response commitments, or did the tier 1 agent fail to tell the client when to expect to be contacted? This type of data really allows you to pinpoint problems, and the survey itself can hardly be construed as overly taxing by your customer. You could even go further and use the same three emoticon buttons on the email response form, but use them under key areas of importance. For example, you could ask the customer to click one of the buttons for each of the following categories: initial wait time, agent, problem resolution, and resolution time. Obviously, each of those areas can be further subdivided, and other areas can be added as well. Keep in mind, though, that less is better if you want good response rates. You can even modify the survey over time, depending on your needs. For example, suppose you change a process or implement some new technology; you could for some period of time add a single question to the survey: "What do you think of our new automated attendant?"

9.2.5 Help Desk Metrics

Your key objectives should come from your efforts to identify what is important to your management, your customers, your peers, your staff, and you. This illustrious group of people are the service center's stakeholders. After creating the list of items that are important to your stakeholders, prioritize them and create a plan (measurable objectives, strategies, and projects) for each item. In addition, identify the data and methodology used to measure and report on each. While your objectives will vary quantitatively from other service centers, and your strategies may be different, their will be a large overlap in the data that all service centers are tracking. Those data are the basis of your key objectives and will allow you to measure your performance from the customers' perspective, the service center's perspective, your company's perspective, and your peers' perspective. Remember, if you can't measure it, you can't manage it, and while the measurements reveal your performance, they also allow you to take corrective action.

The following list of metrics is a compilation of what most service centers are interested in tracking. It is certainly not intended to be a comprehensive list, but is instead a fairly common list. You will want to track additional metrics that support the measurement of your specific plan and objectives. It is also important for you to consider these metrics when you are developing your plan, because they can help you to frame your objectives. For example, when framing objectives regarding costs, you can frame them around the average cost per call, the average cost per workstation supported, or both.

The metrics can be grouped by stakeholder. There are several benefits to grouping your metrics this way. First, it will define the subset of information you need to share with each of the stakeholders. Second, it will help you to define new objectives when working with stakeholders. Finally, it will allow you to review yourself from your stakeholders' perspectives.

In measuring your own performance for the service center stakeholders, you will be interested in gathering the help desk and telephony metrics. These will be centered around

- Call load—the total number of calls and their distribution throughout the day, week, month
- Resolution times by tier and by time interval –(one hour, two hours, etc.)
- Environment
- Response times
- Employees

9.2.6 Call Load

The important call load factors to track are volume and distribution. The hourly distribution is critical so that you can plan your staffing to handle daily peak loads. Peak times may shift (see Figure 9–1), so monitor the trends and make staffing adjustments as necessary. Reviewing the call volume will show you if the number of calls is up or down— but nothing else. It is better to consider volume based on environmental factors, such as number of calls per workstation supported (number of requests divided by number of workstations or customers supported). With this information, you can determine if your volume is up because you are supporting more workstations (or customers) or if it is up for some other reason. If it is up for some other reason, then you should check the volume based on other environmental factors, like the items you have in your subject tree. Identify where the increase has occurred by reviewing the call volumes for the major groupings in your subject tree, and then, if necessary, drill down to subordinate categories. Doing this may lead you to find that, for example, a particular subnet or server is having a recurring problem and is driving your call volume up. With this information, you can initiate an improvement project.

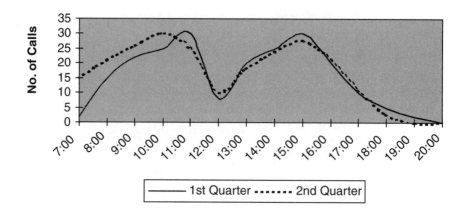

Figure 9–1   Peak load distribution.

9.2.7 Resolution Time

Track the percentage of calls resolved in one hour or less, one to two hours, two to three, and so on (see Figure 9–2). This approach may be more meaningful to you than just tracking your average resolution time. Choose intervals that make sense for you and your service center. You will also want to review resolution times by priority so that you can determine the average resolution time for priority one calls, two, three, and so on. It is also useful to track resolution time based on environmental factors. For example, if you support laptops in your environment, tracking the average resolution time for laptop calls may lead you to developing an improvement project to standardize laptops to reduce the average resolution time. Reviewing the resolution times will point out potential problems that you can investigate further. See Figure 9–3.

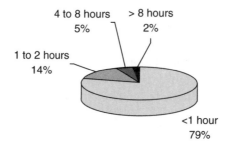

Figure 9–2   Resolution intervals.

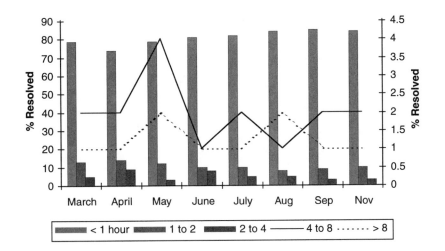

Figure 9–3   Resolution trends.

9.2.8 Environment

Your environment consists of the products you support and the customers who use them. The environment you are supporting, in and of itself, does not provide you with much in terms of metrics. What you are supporting (hardware, software, and clients) may be specifically documented in an asset management tool (if you have one). For the help desk, the environment is usually represented in a subject tree as an abstract of the hardware and software in the environment and client problems and administrative tasks that commonly occur in the environment. When you gather call volumes and resolution times, and organize the data by items in your subject tree, you have an excellent map for finding problems. The more closely your subject tree mirrors your environment, the better the metrics you will be able to gather and the better able you will be to identify and resolve problems. In Figure 9–4, it is obvious that the number of calls for password resets has increased constantly over a 6 month period, while the number of workstations supported has not grown significantly. By looking at the ratio (calls for password resets divided by the number of workstations supported) you can see that the calls per workstation is up, which should cause you to take steps to figure out why and then initiate an improvement project to fix the problem.

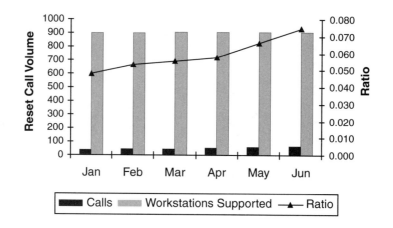

Figure 9–4 Password resets per workstation.

9.2.9 Response Time

Response times are extremely important to your customers, and therefore to you as well. The important items to track are initial and follow-up response times. Depending on your service center, there are several initial response time metrics of importance. For phone calls to the service center, the important metrics are wait time in the queue and abandonment rate. You should review these metrics by time of day so that you can plan your staffing to meet your response time commitments during peak and off peak times. You can only gather this information if your telephone system supports this function. If your customers can contact you for support via some other method, such as email or fax, it is important to track how long it takes to respond to those customers. In all of these cases, you should at a minimum have internal commitments, and you may have external commitments to your customers in the form of SLAs. Keep a close watch on these trends to make sure that you are meeting and continue to meet your commitments. The sample chart in Figure 9–5 shows the average response time in seconds, the abandonment rate, and the call volumes on an hourly basis. This information will help you plan your staffing levels.

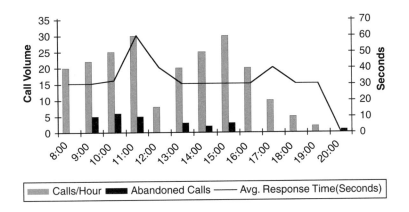

Figure 9–5   Response time metrics.

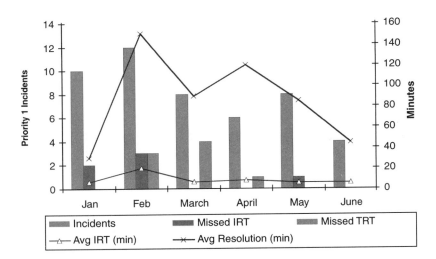

Figure 9–6   Response performance for the tier 2 hardware support resource pool.

In addition to the initial contacts with the customer, you should keep track of the time it takes to make follow-up contacts. This is extremely important because you may have made a verbal commitment or may have an SLA, and in either case, the customer will certainly have an expectation of when he or she will receive a follow-up contact from the service center if the call was not resolved during the initial contact.

This is even more important to track when you route or escalate a contact to an outside vendor or a support group outside of the help desk or service center. If you route or escalate to a group that is outside of your direct control, they can seriously damage your relationship with the customer if they provide a substandard response.

Figure 9–6 summarizes the response performance for the tier 2 hardware support resource pool. The information shows, among other things, their average initial response time (IRT) for priority 1 incidents. It also shows, by month, the number of priority 1 incidents for which they did not achieve their target IRT. TRT is target resolution time and, like IRT, is shown in minutes.

9.2.10 Employees

There are two types of employee metrics to track. Obviously, you want metrics to review employees' performance. It is also very beneficial to survey your employees regarding their opinions of their own performance and of the service center's performance. The typical metrics to gather regarding the employees' performance will come from your help desk software and your telephony software. These include number of calls or problems opened and number of calls or problems closed. You will have a target for the service center in terms of calls handled at the initial point of contact, and that target will be imposed on your service center staff. Use these metrics to see if your staff are achieving the targets. As with any metrics, though, you can't look at these in isolation. These metrics will not tell you why a particular agent isn't hitting his or her targets, and they won't tell you if the customer is delighted. For example, at one service center, the service center representatives knew rate of problems closed was a key measure in their evaluations. One individual had a phenomenal close rate, but he achieved it by sacrificing all common courtesies to the customers—who despised him. In another case, the individual was not meeting the target closure rate because he was routing far to many calls to the tier 2 support teams—calls that should have been handled and closed at tier 1. Not only did this delay a resolution for the customer, it wasted the time of tier 2 resources.

Another important measure is average call length. Most service centers have established time limits per call. The call is then routed or escalated, usually based on priority. The time limit will vary dramatically, depending on your call volume, the number of resources available, the complexity of calls, the service model, and your customers' tolerance for waiting in the call queue.

Table 9–1   Example Employee Service Utilization Metrics

Employee	Scheduled time(min)	Ready Time (min)	Calls Taken	Talk Time (min)	Hold Time (min)	Wait Time (min)	Talk Ratio	Average Call Length (min)	Scheduled vs. Ready
Bob	390	392	30	232	40	120	69%	12.6	2
John	390	380	10	308	32	40	89%	37.5	(10)

Employee service utilization metrics are important as well. If you have the tools, gather the data to see how much of the tier 1 staffs' time was actually spent providing service. To do this, you must have six basic metrics available: the scheduled phone time, the talk time, the hold time, the ready time, the wait time, and the number of calls taken. The scheduled phone time is the number of minutes you planned for an employee to be available on the phone. Let's assume an 8-hour shift minus a 1-hour lunch and two 15-minute breaks, for a total scheduled time of 390 minutes. The ready time is the actual amount of time an agent is logged into the call distribution system and ready to take calls. It is good to compare the scheduled phone time with the ready time because it could indicate one of the biggest problems faced by help desk management—tardiness. After evaluating these metrics, you may find that you need to speak with chronically tardy individuals, or that 390 minutes is simply unrealistic for your service center. The talk time is the actual amount of time the agent is on the phone with the customer. The hold time is the amount of time the agent has calls on hold, and the wait time is the time between calls (waiting for a call to be routed), which is calculated as ready time minus talk time minus hold time. With these basic metrics, you can calculate talk ratio, which indicates how much time was spent on the phone with customers compared to the amount of ready time. It is calculated as the talk time plus the hold time divided by the ready time. This ratio indicates the amount of time an agent was working versus waiting for calls to come in. You would expect this number to be consistent across all employees, but that may not be the case. If it isn't, look at the number of calls each person has received. The agent who takes more calls will have more wait time, and thus his or her talk time ratio may be lower than that of an agent who takes fewer calls. Why? As shown in Table 9–1, assuming the average wait time between calls is 4 minutes and Bob took 30 calls during the day, he had 30 intervals of wait time between calls, for a total wait time of 120 minutes. If John took only 10 calls during the day, his total wait time was only 40 minutes, assuming he was on the phone all day with the 10 calls he handled. While John's talk ratio looks much better than Bob's, a closer look shows that Bob handled far more calls than John, and therefore John's average call length must be significantly higher than Bob's. You can calculate each employee's average time per call by adding their total talk time and hold time and then dividing by the number of calls. This should lead you to evaluate John's calls. Is John's average call length always high, or is this just a one-time occurrence? If they are always higher, you need to find out if John needs additional training or if he is spending too much time socializing with customers. You can use these basic metrics to evaluate an employee's performance, as long as you don't look at any one metric in isolation. Keep in mind that even if you look at all of the metrics described and the employee seems to have exemplary performance, these metrics will not indicate anything about the customer's experience with the employee.

You can also gather valuable information by surveying your service center employees. As with customer surveys, determining the frequency is important. Unlike customer surveys, you should get nearly 100 percent response. The typical questions are

- Do you have the tools you need to do your job?
- Do you have the training you need?
- Is your workload reasonable?
- Are you satisfying your customers?
- Are you achieving your targets?
- Are other service center support tiers responsive?
- Are other support tiers impacting your ability to meet customer commitments?
- Are there recurring problems in the customer environment that should be fixed?
- What additional training do our customers need?
- How can we reduce call volume?
- What changes can we make in our processes to improve your ability to satisfy our customers?
- Have you gone the "extra mile" to help a customer? Describe.

- Have you gone the "extra mile" to help the service center? Describe.
- Are there any special projects you would like to undertake?

Make sure you publish the results of your survey and your action plan to address the problems and suggestions. For example, show a list of tools requested and the percentage of respondents that requested the tool. Describe what you are planning to do about it. If there is nothing you can do about it, then state so and explain why. If respondents have issues with the other support levels, make sure they are real problems, not misguided expectations, and take appropriate action. The action could include a process change, updates to an SLA, or a new SLA between support groups, depending on the problem. This is invaluable information because it gives you inside information on required improvement projects, performance, customers, and working relationships, and it provides you with documentation for performance reviews. If you follow up on the recommendations from the survey, you can improve morale and foster a terrific team environment. Assignment of special projects can also have a very positive effect on morale. First, the project is probably one that you need to have completed. Second, it gives the employee a chance to accomplish a task that is outside of his or her normal responsibilities, and often outside of normal work hours. These projects can include root cause analysis, troubleshooting unusual problems, product research and evaluation, writing for the knowledge base, computer-based training, and more.

9.2.11 Process-Specific Metrics

You can and should review metrics associated with your problem management processes. These metrics will allow you to see if the processes are being followed and will also show you if there are weaknesses or areas for improvement in the processes.

Routing and Escalation

Specifically, you should identify data to keep track of your routing and escalation processes. Your routing and escalation processes have a dramatic impact on the service center. They impact your costs, resolution times, customer satisfaction, service center employee morale, and your

SLAs. When a call is routed or escalated, additional resources and additional time are involved. Within most service centers, each successive tier within the center has more expensive resources, thus potentially driving up the cost for that problem. This is particularly inefficient if tier 2 is handling tier 1 overflow. Calls that are escalated usually take longer, and the customer usually has to explain the issue again, which can reduce his or her level of satisfaction. When calls that should be handled at one tier are regularly routed to the next successive tier, the receiving tier can become frustrated, and over time, respect and cooperation between the tiers will diminish.

Keep track of the number of problems being escalated. Figure 9–7 shows the total number of problem tickets escalated to each tier and Figure 9–8 shows the percentage of problem tickets escalated to each tier. If there is an increasing number of problems being escalated or routed from one tier to the next, you need to take action before the volume overwhelms your capability to deliver service. First, you need to review the items being routed to determine if they were legitimately routed. If they were not legitimate, then you must figure out what happened. Is it a training issue at the help desk? Are calls being routed because the volume coming into the service center has exceeded the tier 1 capacity?

You should also check to make sure that problems are being routed to the appropriate groups. You can really blow your SLA commitments when calls are sent to the wrong resource pool, where they can languish until they are sent to the correct resource pool. If the problem happens frequently, it can have a very negative impact on morale, because the receiving group will lose confidence in the sending group or in management. This can be difficult information to gather because typically there is no way to document the event. One approach to consider is adding an optional field to the ticket, such as a checkbox, that the receiving support group can simply check when they have received the ticket in error. With these metrics, you can gather information on the frequency of occurrence and begin to troubleshoot the issue. The problem can occur for a number of reasons, but typical reasons include

- The sender misdiagnosed the problem.
- The sender didn't know the appropriate place to send the problem.
- Organizational changes occurred without realignment of the help desk routing.

- Only one company expert is available for a particular problem, and that expert can never seem to get away from support, even when it is no longer his or her responsibility.

- A new support problem has occurred, and no one has been assigned responsibility.

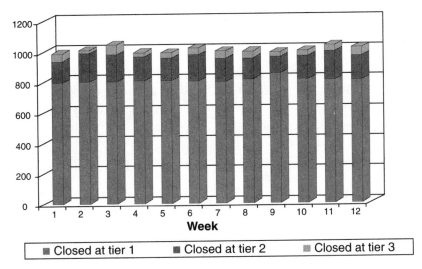

Figure 9–7 An example of the number of problems escalated by tier.

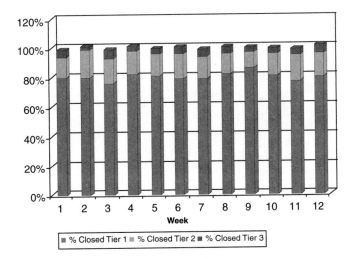

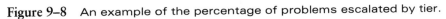

Figure 9–8 An example of the percentage of problems escalated by tier.

Priority Assignment

You should review the number of tickets at each priority level and pay particular attention to the number of priority 1 and 2 tickets. If necessary, you should review the priority 1 tickets to see if the priority level is being correctly applied. Because you have time commitments associated with priority levels, the incorrect application of priorities can have a dramatic impact on your costs and customer satisfaction. Analysis of problems may reveal the need to train customers on the application of priorities, the need to train the service center staff, or in many cases, both. An analysis of unusually high numbers of priority 1 and 2 calls at one service center revealed that the center had an informal policy of providing priority 1 and 2 levels of service to the company executives and their assistants. While this was a politically motivated strategy, analysis showed that the strategy created significant unnecessary costs. This type of priority treatment was expected by the executives, so the service center had no choice but to comply. To separate these metrics from their regular priority 1 calls, the service center created a special priority level, 1e, specifically for use with the executive staff. Calls from anyone on the special handling list received the 1e priority and the same level of service as any priority 1 call. This was a good approach for the service center because it allowed them to gather metrics about what it was costing the corporation to provide that level of support. It also allowed the service center to separate those costs and metrics out so they could compare "normal" operations with their peer companies, which were not providing priority services to their executives. An additional benefit was that the service center could show the executives what it cost to provide that level of service on a cost per executive workstation versus cost per corporate workstation basis and let management decide if the special treatment should be continued.

An alternative, and perhaps a better approach, is to develop and implement an SLA with the executive staff.

Technician Dispatch

Another process benchmark to monitor is the number of times that technicians are dispatched to the customers' desktop. Dispatching technicians is expensive because of the time wasted traveling, even if it is only to another floor. Tracking this information is particularly useful if you have an alternative to dispatching, such as remote control tools. A technician with a remote control tool can resolve more problems than a dispatched technician (excluding hardware problems). Often, technicians would rather go out on tour, so you should monitor this closely. Remote control tools, used correctly, are a terrific way to lower your operating costs and improve efficiency.

Knowledge Base Usage

If you are fortunate enough to have a knowledge base, keep track of its usage. If the knowledge base is not being used, then it is highly likely that your staff are repeatedly troubleshooting the same problems, and potentially implementing inconsistent solutions. Some service centers insist that the knowledge base be searched or referenced for every support call, even if the staff know the problem and the solution. This may seem silly, but there are good reasons to implement this strategy. One reason is to ensure that the same workaround or solution is implemented every time. Another is that the knowledge base is used as the communication tool for new workarounds or solutions.

If you have taken the time to define and implement processes, you should put forth the effort to ensure they are being followed and to measure their effectiveness. Your processes must change over time to keep up with changes in your business. Measuring your processes allows you to proactively make incremental changes. The business you are supporting will change steadily and incrementally. If you are not also incrementally changing your processes to support the business changes, the compounded effect of the business changes will eventually impact your ability to provide support. Incremental changes are much easier than major process changes to implement.

9.2.12 Management Metrics

No matter what type of service center you run, you will obviously want to focus on your costs and cost effectiveness, and certainly your management will be interested in this information as well. Often, management stakeholders do not know enough about service centers to even know what information to ask for. This is your chance to educate them. If the only number they have ever seen is your total annual operating cost and capital budgets, the sooner you educate them, the better. They will know that they are spending a lot of money, but will have no idea if it is being used wisely. If your service center generates revenue, then your management is much more likely to be in touch with your performance than if your service center is strictly overhead. If you generate revenue through the sale of training, or charge customers on a per call or service plan basis, it is likely that you report financials just like any other company profit center. Management can understand that type of reporting. If you're not a profit center, then you should compare your costs to that of your peers. One of the best metrics to use is your cost per workstation supported versus those costs in other service centers. Just make sure you are comparing apples to apples. This is your total operating costs divided by the number of workstations you support. When calculating your total costs, make sure you include the following components:

- Salaries plus loaded benefits
- Software support charges
- Hardware support charges
- Facilities such as rent and utilities
- Telecommunications charges
- Leases, if you lease your service center equipment
- Outsourced support activities
- Independent contractors and consultants
- Training
- Office supplies
- Memberships
- Subscriptions
- Conferences
- Other allocations of corporate costs

Make sure you include any and all operating costs that are necessary for you to run your service center. If you are not sure what to include, ask your accounting or finance department for assistance. Be careful, though, not to include costs that are not necessarily yours. For example, if for some reason you budget and pay for the entire corporation's network operating costs, then make sure you benchmark against companies that do the same; otherwise, do not include those costs (other than the costs of your own subnet) in your calculations.

Another calculation that may be of value to you and your management team is cost per direct service provider. That is, take the total of all of the costs previously listed and divide that sum by the number of people on your staff who provide direct support to the customer. Since you're a manager, you should *not* be counted as providing direct support, but your salary should still be included as overhead. This information will help you keep track of and identify changes in overhead.

You can also use your total cost information to calculate your average cost per minute of service provided. To calculate your average cost per minute of support time, divide your total costs by the total number of minutes of support. Needless to say, this can be a misleading number, because it is difficult to determine the number of minutes of support time. If you just consider the total number of minutes from the time a problem ticket was opened until the time it was closed, you may be adding minutes that did not include actual support time. This inevitably occurs when tickets are routed to other groups, because of the lag time until the other group takes action and the potential for lag time between the time the problem was fixed and the time the ticket was closed. If your system allows you to track the actual work time, though, this would be a terrific metric for charging support, based on actual usage, back to the clients. This approach would be more accurate than charging back support based on the number of workstations supported, because it would more accurately reflect the amount of work done for each client. A side benefit of this approach is that customers may call less frequently for nonlegitimate support if they know they are being charged on a per-minute basis.

There are other benefits to knowing your costs on a per-minute basis. If, for example, you could track the number of minutes spent supporting a particular product, you could easily calculate the cost to support that product and then use standard cost/benefit analysis to evaluate and justify improvement projects.

Another measure often used is the average cost per call. This metric is really only useful when you consider it as a trend. When you evaluate it as a trend, it gives you general information about your costs to your ratio of calls, and thus may indicate that your overhead is increasing. This metric, though, is not necessarily a meaningful measurement, because it fails to consider call complexity, type of service provided, and legitimacy of calls. Consider, for example, company ABC, which sells software for processing natural gas measurement charts. Their product has been on the market for over 10 years and their customers are highly trained specialists in the gas measurement field. The support calls received by ABC are highly technical and the questions are business–related, consultative usage questions. These calls can take anywhere from 15 minutes to several days to resolve. ABC's service model is to provide whatever level of support it takes to service the customer. ABC receives far fewer calls and spends much more time on each of those calls than a typical help desk. An evaluation of their average cost per call would appear to be atrocious at $150. Now consider company XYZ, which has an average cost per call of $49. While it appears that XYZ is incredibly efficient, a closer inspection reveals that 18 percent of the calls included in the average were not considered to be legitimate calls, but were simple training-related calls that could have been avoided had the customers attended the introductory PC course required for all staff. If the baseline number of calls was 1,000, then XYZ's actual cost per call would be more like $59.75 per call ($49,000 total costs per month divided by 820 legitimate calls). This calculation does not factor in the cost of 180 nonlegitimate calls. You could calculate, instead, 180 nonlegitimate calls at an average $49 per call to equal $8,820 spent on nonlegitimate calls.

Average cost per call is a common measure used in the industry. If you are planning to measure your own and benchmark against others, make sure the benchmarks you use are based on a similar business model of similar size, and include in the calculations as many other similarities in terms of costs as you can find.

▶ 9.3 Formal Review of Metrics

Now that the metrics have been defined, and assuming that you are collecting them, someone has to review them. As the manager of the service center, you need to identify who will review the metrics and how often. For each metric, or most likely, each set of metrics (a report), you must define four things. First, you need to decide who owns the performance represented by the metrics. For example, the employee performance metrics would be owned by the shift supervisor and the employees working that shift. The shift supervisor has primary responsibility for the performance of all the employees in his or her shift. Second, you need to work with the performance owner to determine the required frequency for reviewing the metrics. This ensures that if you are not reviewing the metrics, someone else is—and is placing the appropriate emphasis on those metrics. For a large help desk, the shift supervisor should review the employee performance statistics daily, and you may want only a weekly summary. Third, you need to develop a communication plan for each set of metrics. The communication plan details who should get a copy of the report, what format the report is in, and what subset of data is included for each recipient. Fourth, the communication plan should include the frequency for sending or posting the report, which will probably vary by recipient (stakeholder). You may want to receive a summary level of the report on a weekly or monthly basis, while the detailed daily version and the weekly summary version are both posted on the wall of fame near the help desk for all help desk participants to see. The performance owner is also responsible for executing the communication plan.

To organize this information, you should develop a number of matrices. One matrix should list the metrics and the performance owner for each metric and indicate the frequency with which performance owners must review the metrics. This will clearly communicate performance responsibility to your staff. Another useful matrix is one that lists the metrics and the stakeholders that wish to review them, as well as the frequency of review. This will essentially be the beginning of your communication plan—only the beginning, because it indicates metrics, not reports. Once you have determined which metrics each stakeholder is going to review and the reporting frequency, you can create reporting templates to meet those requirements.

Create another matrix that documents the metrics and the reporting templates and indicates which metrics are included in each report. You could organize the report templates as column headings, showing the daily reports first, then the weekly, monthly, quarterly, and annual.

Finally, create a matrix that shows the reports and the stakeholders and indicates which reports should be sent to each stakeholder and how often (e.g., weekly, monthly). This matrix is your communication plan for reports.

It is a good idea to create similar matrices for meetings, which indicate the meeting date, the frequency, the attendees, and the reports that will be reviewed.

Why go to the trouble of creating so much documentation? There are many good reasons. First, this documentation allows you to keep track of what is important to the service center stakeholders and continually reinforces how they will be reviewing your performance. Second, it communicates that information to your service center employees. It is extremely important that the employees know what is important to customers and management, and how those stakeholders will be reviewing their performance. This information keeps the service center and its stakeholders synchronized on what is important. Third, when you conduct review meetings, the meetings tend to be more focused because all attendees know what will be reviewed. Fourth, it allows you to take a vacation, because you can communicate to your temporary replacement what he or she should be reviewing and what meetings should be held. Fifth, it allows you to periodically review the reporting requirements with stakeholders and eliminate reporting that is no longer required, as well as add new information as necessary.

You should review the reporting requirements with the stakeholders every 6 months. This should be a simple and quick review to check that the metrics they are receiving are still appropriate. You should organize your metrics by frequency (daily, weekly, monthly, quarterly), and then review the ones they currently receive. Cross off the ones they are no longer interested in and check anything new they want to receive. You could also do this on a report basis instead of a metric basis if you want to reduce the number of custom reports.

▶ 9.4 Key Roles and Management Teams

The responsibilities of the coordinator are to establish and maintain the service metrics, chair the problem review team and supporting processes, and ensure problem management processes and communications are running efficiently. The key objectives are to

1. Identify and resolve problems that affect the performance of the service center.
2. Resolve tickets in exception status.

9.4.1 Ticket Exception Review Team

A team with responsibility for ticket exceptions should meet daily or, at least, weekly, depending on volume, to ensure that a backlog of open tickets does not grow out of control. The team is responsible for review of all requests in exception status. Tickets in exception status are requests that are still open beyond their target resolution or fulfillment time. The goal of the team is to take action to close the tickets and identify reasons that the tickets have remained open. Analyzing the reason tickets have remained open may lead to the discovery of process problems, ownership problems, root causes, training issues, and so on.

The team should include the service center manager and the resource pool owners. The resource pool owners should be members of this team because they will own many of the tickets in exception status. You may elect to have only the pool owners with tickets on the exception list attend exception status meetings.

If the service center manager does not participate as a member of the team, someone who has enough authority to ensure that the resource pool managers continue to work diligently on their backlog of problems should be on the team.

9.4.2 Problem Management Process Review Team

The problem management process review team (process team) should focus its efforts primarily on the successes, or lack of successes, of the service center's processes. This focus is absolutely critical if the service center is to be all it can be. The process team should fully expect resistance to implementing new processes or changing existing processes from all tiers of the service center, particularly given that new or changed processes initially increase workload and often add accountability.

This team should consist of the process owners, who may be the same group that reviews ticket exceptions, and the resource pool owners. On a regular basis—weekly is recommended if you're implementing new processes—the team should review and address all process-related reports. If you are not implementing new processes, the team can review process metrics less frequently. The team should address any process issues that impact the center's ability to deliver services. The team may also monitor and report on implemented changes. If the pool owners are not the primary team members, they should at least be involved in or receive periodic updates. In addition to periodic measurements and problem exceptions, the group should continuously focus on and monitor interdepartmental relationships, ensuring appropriate cooperation and collaboration.

These meetings must *not* focus on specific technology issues that result in trouble tickets. The entire focus of the meeting is service center processes. Items that should be addressed in the meeting include initial response times, escalation (what is working and what is not), responsibilities, ownership, and other such issues.

There are many different ways of fine-tuning the service center processes that the process team can focus on. The items considered big-ticket items are

- Knowledge base
- Escalation
- Root cause
- Special handling list
- Initial response time
- Adding and removing services

These major items, discussed in the following sections, must be working well before there is any need to even consider fine-tuning. When these processes are working efficiently, the service center will be well on its way to achieving customer satisfaction and reducing its costs.

Knowledge Base

The process team should review at its weekly meetings the success of the knowledge capture process. The team should focus on where the process is working and where it is not. It is anticipated that certain groups or individuals will be "too busy" to create reports or to review and approve reports. This is particularly true if you are implementing a knowledge base for the first time and your staff have yet to adopt the knowledge culture.

The team should review the quality of the reports being created. This is often a difficult issue to address, but these reports should be of high enough quality to show your customers. The team should also monitor the growth and usage of the knowledge base to determine whether or not the process is being followed. It is absolutely true that it will take a significant amount of time to build the knowledge base. It is also true that if done correctly, it will be well worth the up-front costs because it should increase the number of problems resolved at tier 1 and tier 2, which should make the customer happier and reduce overall service center costs. This process is initially intensive because it takes the back-log of knowledge out of the technicians' heads and institutionalizes it in the database.

Escalation

The process team must review in its weekly meetings the percentage of issues escalated from tier to tier. These metrics should be reviewed by problem type to identify if problems that shouldn't be escalated are being escalated. The team should also review to see if tickets are being escalated to the correct resource pool.

A careful review of escalation may identify opportunities to decrease the number of items escalated. Generally, that means moving a service usually provided by tier 2 to tier 1, or from tier 3 to tier 2. The team should look for patterns and opportunities to resolve more issues at tier 1. When a service is found that could be moved to tier 1, someone should be designated to create a proposal and make recommendations to the process team. The proposal should document what would be required to handle that type of issue at tier 1 and should include items such as training and tools required, estimated costs, benefits, and a project schedule. The team would then approve or disapprove the com-mitment required to move the service.

Root Cause

The process team should review the work of the person or persons responsible for identifying and resolving root cause problems. The team should focus on problems that create a significant number of ser-vice center requests and high-priority problems. They should also review the status of identifying the root cause and the status of resolv-ing the root problem.

Special Handling List

The process team should maintain a special handling list of customers (executives, for example) that receive special treatment when they con-tact the service center. The team should review this list at least once a month. The objective is to add or remove names to the list as required, and the discussion should not take more than a few minutes. The list and its implications to response time must be known to all agents within the service center; otherwise, those customers may not receive the service levels they are guaranteed or that they expect.

Initial Response Time

The process team should review initial response time by pool and take corrective action when necessary. This could include either modifying the IRT commitments or correcting bad behavior or some root cause.

Adding and Removing Services

The process team should review proposals brought forth by the service center employees to add or remove services from the service center's offering list. The important factor for adding services is preparedness to support the new offering. The important factor for removing a service is customer impact and acceptance. Standard templates and processes should be used to develop proposals to add and remove services. For more information, see Chapter 3, "Maintaining a Service Catalog."

▶ 9.5 Reports

There are nearly infinite variations of reports that can be generated from a basic list of metrics. Depending on management priority, they can be organized to review the service center's overall costs, effectiveness, operations, and personnel. When goals are established in each of these key areas, the metrics can be used to manage the service center. As you move forward and continue to modify the services your center provides, other reports will become necessary. Once a base of metric data is established, you can use that data to negotiate service levels.

9.5.1 Baseline Data

As already mentioned, one of the keys to your success will be creating measurable objectives that lead to some sort of benefit to your company, either reduced costs, increased revenues, or improved service levels. To establish those measurable benefits, you must have baseline data to measure against. That is, you must know where you are to accurately state where you are going and when you will be there. If you don't have any baseline data, or if what you have is not thorough or reliable, then one of your first projects should be to establish baseline data. This is not a trivial task and should not be underestimated.

9.5.2 Performance Targets

A basic set of reports is required when the service center first comes online. The basic reports might be "canned" reports that already exist in your service center's system. Keep in mind that most companies that produce and sell service center software provide that software to many other clients. When it comes to reporting, you get the benefit of standard reports that most of the vendor's clients use. If you're not sure what reports to use when you are just getting started, use these canned reports to review overall performance of the service center. Once a performance baseline is established, use the data to develop performance goals.

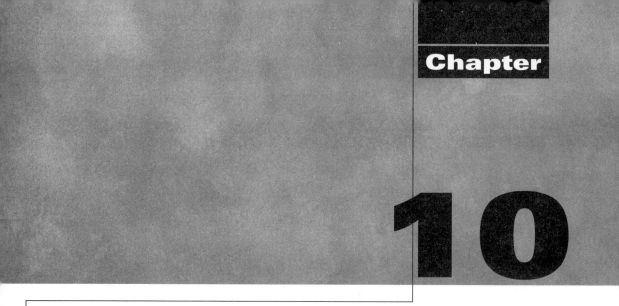

Service Level Agreements

A service level agreement (SLA) is a contract between a service provider and a service receiver. The contract usually describes the services that will be provided, the quality or level of the services, and the responsibilities of both the service requestor and the service provider. SLAs may or may not include service pricing. The agreement will also specify a means of measuring each party's compliance to the agreed upon terms. There are two broad categories of SLAs: internal and external. External SLAs always seem to be more formal and carry more weight than their internal counterparts, because it is unlikely that two parties within the same company will sue each other. Internal SLAs should be treated just as seriously as external SLAs, because customer satisfaction is at stake.

A typical service center will have multiple SLAs. The service center may have one or more SLAs with its customers. In some cases, the service center will have a separate SLA with each customer group. For these SLAs, the service center is the service provider.

The service center may also have SLAs in which it is the service receiver. This is typical when the service center relies on third-party support, such as hardware support. The service center should have SLAs with each organization that it relies on for support but does not directly manage. For example, suppose the network operations group provides tier 3 support to the service center but is not managed by the service center. The network operations group has a full-time job operating the network. It is likely that resolving service center requests is lower on their priority list than their regular job. An SLA should be established between network operations and the service center that documents each party's commitments. This is critical because for you to commit a response time to your customer, you must sometimes rely on the network operations group to resolve the problem for you. Without the SLA, problems may go unresolved for long periods.

Figure 10–1 shows a map of SLAs in a fictitious service center. The core service center box represents the tier 1 and tier 2 employees and contractors that are dedicated full-time to the service center and are directly managed by the service center. In this example, there is only one SLA with the customers, but there could be more. The other SLAs show where the service center is the service receiver. Notice that the services come from both internal and external teams.

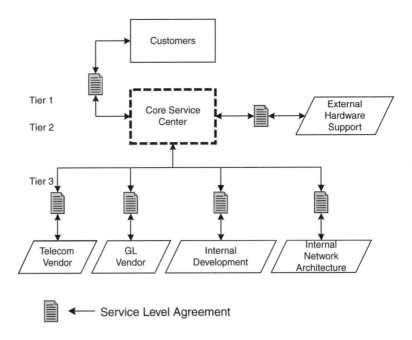

Figure 10–1 Service level agreement map.

SLAs are critical to your success but can be very difficult to set up, maintain, and monitor. The process for creating an SLA is very similar to negotiating a contract. Drafts are created and reviewed by both parties. Items are clarified and modified in the draft, and then reviewed again. This process iterates until all parties agree on the terms. You must have metrics to create an SLA, because you must establish and agree on targets. For example, a typical term in an SLA would be that 90 percent of calls to the service center will be answered in 40 seconds or less. If you do not have these metrics, you have no way of knowing if you can achieve that objective. This leads to some general guidelines about creating SLAs.

1. Make sure that the targets are realistic. An SLA is a contract that each party must live up to.

2. If you can't measure it, don't include it in the SLA.

3. Make sure the service center has SLAs in place with all of its service providers (the people who support you) *before* negotiating an SLA with the service center's customers.

4. Be as specific as possible about everything added to the SLA to make sure there are no misunderstandings or misinterpretations.

5. Attorneys will be involved when you are negotiating external SLAs. If you are having difficulty reaching agreement on an internal SLA, an internal company lawyer can be helpful both as an arbiter and in clarifying language.

▶ 10.1 SLA Content

Whether you are the service provider or the service receiver, the content of an SLA is very similar. All service center-related SLAs should contain the following information:

1. The names of the parties involved.

2. Primary contact information.

3. The term of the agreement, typically one year.

4. The hours of operation and availability.

5. The services to be provided. Don't forget that availability for particular services can vary by time. When this is the case, make sure you document which services are available at which times. Be specific!

6. A separate list of services for which special fees apply.

7. Methods available for the customer to contact the service center during normal business hours and after-hour options.

8. Definitions of request priorities and response times for both immediate and managed service models.

9. Definition of escalation procedures and response times for both immediate and managed service models.

10. The service requestor's (customer's) responsibilities, such as what not to call for, what to do before calling, any mandatory training, responding to surveys, and so on.

11. A list of the service level metrics and the agreed upon targets.

12. Any applicable support fees not covered on a service-by-service basis. For example, you may charge $100 per month for each workstation supported under this agreement.

13. Formal review cycles to review performance against targets. Be specific about how often the reviews will occur, who will attend, and what metrics will be reviewed.

14. A list of report templates that will be distributed for review, as well as a list of people who will receive the report and the reporting frequency.

15. A list of other components supported (other than addressed in the list of services provided).

16. Procedures for terminating the agreement or for taking corrective action in the case of failure of one party to uphold its contractual obligations.

You can organize the SLA according to this list, or you can modify it to combine information on a service-by-service basis. For example, you could list each service as a section or subsection on its own. Within the section for the service, you could list the hours of availability for the service, any applicable fees, the metrics that will be used to measure the performance, the performance targets, customer responsibility for that service, and any other information applicable to that service. Instead of a service-by-service approach, you could also use groups of services where the important attributes are the same.

▶ 10.2 Using the SLA

Now that you have an SLA you must use it. All to often, they sit and gather dust for a year until it's time to renew them. This is true for both internal and external agreements and is indicative of a service center that is not under control. If you don't have SLAs, or if you have them but are not monitoring them, you cannot measure and control your performance.

Measure your actual performance against the targets in the agreement you have with your customers. You need to do this even if your customers don't care. If you have fallen short somewhere, you need to take corrective action. Find the problem and initiate an improvement project. Address the issue with your customer and tell the customer how you plan to fix it. Review your customers' performance against their commitments in the agreement and help them initiate improvement projects where necessary.

Use the same approach for the agreements in which you are the service receiver. Evaluate both parties' performance and take corrective action where necessary. You should review performance on a monthly basis so that you can be proactive and incrementally improve performance.

When you take a proactive approach to managing performance, you should expect performance to improve—both the performance you are able to provide your customers and the performance of your suppliers. These improvements, or higher expectations, should be included when you renew the SLA. In other words, keep raising the bar. For example, suppose you negotiated a service level with your customer that said you would service 85 percent of the requests during the initial contact. At the end of the year, you had actually achieved 87 percent. When you renew the agreement, you should set the service level target at 87 percent. Constant improvement should be your goal. There will obviously be some cases where it would not be economically feasible to increase performance, but this should be the exception rather than the rule.

Service Center Tools

More and more companies are recognizing that the service center is critical to their success. They are placing much more emphasis on the service centers' mission to keep their own employees productive, and they are realizing the value good customer service has to their bottom line. To provide better service at a lower cost, and to reduce downtime and lost productivity, service centers must rely on and invest in technology. The service center product market is therefore thriving, and new and improved products are coming to the market every day.

There are many different tools available that can help your service center provide better service to your customers and also help you to reduce costs and improve efficiency. In this chapter, we will take a broad look across four categories of tools. We will discuss tools that your customers will use to access the service center. Access tools make it easier for your customers to contact the service center to get the information they need, while giving you efficient control over the process. We will discuss the plethora of tools and technology now available to help you deliver your services to the customer. These tools can help you deliver services more cost effectively. We will discuss tools that can proactively notify the service center of problems or potential problems. Finally, we will discuss customer-enabling tools. Enabling tools allow customers to help themselves. Some of the tools we will discuss fall into more than one of these categories. For example, an interactive voice response

(IVR) system can serve as a service delivery tool and as a customer-enabling tool.

Purchasing tools is no guarantee of success. With so many products and vendors in the marketplace, it is difficult to make tool choices. There are four key factors you should consider when selecting a tool: the product technology, the market strength of the vendor, open interface standards and policy, and the vendor's strategy for the future. Look for tool technology that fits into your standard, or planned, environment. You don't want to buy a tool that uses completely different technology than you currently support or plan to support in the future. Make sure the technology the tool uses can meet your current and future needs—that it is scalable and flexible. There are many vendors in the market, so a shakeout is likely. Tools are a significant investment, so you need to make sure your vendor will be around to support you. While there may be benefits to selecting smaller firms, there are also risks. Consider selecting a market leader, because they are most likely to survive and thrive. Look for a vendor that has enough strength in the marketplace to be viable for the future. Look for a vendor that has an open strategy for integration with other tools. An integrated tool set from one vendor is certainly valuable, but you want to have the ability to choose the best tools for your environment, which often means integrating one vendor's tools with another's. A good vendor with an open integration policy will have the ability to seamlessly integrate with the best ancillary tools available. As an example, if you want to integrate your problem management system (PMS) with your desktop management system (DMS), make sure your PMS has that capability. Finally, evaluate the vendor's strategy for the future. Just because the vendor is a market leader today, with the technology and the open integration policy you desire, does not guarantee that it will hold that place in the future. Suppose your PMS vendor decides to build its own DMS. Future versions of their PMS may not support your chosen DMS, which could be a huge problem for you. Further, we've all seen market leaders stumble by resting on their laurels or by making bad business decisions, so it is important to evaluate the vendor's strategy for the future.

To be of value, tools must have the ability to do what you intend them to do, and you have to know how to use them. Tool implementations succeed or fail for a number of different reasons. To ensure that your company makes a wise investment in tools, you should follow a few basic steps.

- Are you going to automate your existing processes, or do they need to be revised? If your processes need revision, you should revise them *prior* to choosing a tool. While this increases your lead time, you will be far better off in the long run. Automating inadequate processes gives you automated inadequate processes. The new processes are criteria that help you to choose the best tool for your needs.

- Identify the business need for the tool. Are there organizational problems that can be resolved by implementing this tool? Can this tool bring escalating costs under control? Are customers unhappy about any area of service? What is the business need that you plan to support through the use of tools?

- Identify the goals and objectives. What tasks do you want your tools to accomplish? Make sure you develop a complete set of your requirements and never let a tool vendor do this for you. Document the mandatory requirements, the preferred requirements, and the optional requirements.

- Identify one or more solutions. Solutions can include both manual solutions and new tool solutions. Closely evaluate tools against your requirements document and create a short list of tools and vendors. Identify and price alternative solutions. Make sure you include training and implementation support.

- Create a cost/benefit analysis for each alternative solution.

- Check references and visit sites that are using the products under consideration. Talk to the users to find out about the tool and the vendor. Where is the tool weak? Has the vendor provided good support? Is the vendor responsive? What is the vendor's plan for the future? Verify any assumptions that are based on claims from the vendor. Tell the site users how you plan to use the tool and ask them to tell you where you may run into difficulties.

- Choose the appropriate solution. Ask for a trial if the solution is a new product.

- Monitor the implementation and usage. Take corrective action where necessary.

- Measure your actual return against your cost/benefit analysis.

Too many tool investments fail because there was no money for training or implementation support. Service center tools are complex, and you will need training and support. Often, the tools end up not being integrated, and therefore their true value is not realized. Make sure you have budgeted for training and integration support. If you have network monitoring tools but they are not integrated with the problem management software, you are missing out on significant benefits. Make sure you have buy-in from the people who are supposed to use the tools. Too often, tools fail because people don't want to use them. A good example is remote control tools, which both the technician and the customer may resist.

▶ 11.1 Access Tools

Access tools are the tools your customers will use to contact the service center. Certainly the most common method, both past and present, has been the telephone. This is changing, though, as more companies are using Web gateways and networks (both intranets and the Internet), as a method to allow customers to contact the service center. The use of the telephone as an access method will not go away, at least not anytime soon, but there are compelling reasons to augment access by using computer-to-computer access technology.

There are very mature and robust telephone access tools available today. These tools make telephone contact with the service center very efficient and effective, while improving the accessibility for your customers. These tools also gather metrics for you that let you track your service center's performance.

11.1.1 Automated Call Distribution System

The automated call distribution (ACD) system is a combination of telephony hardware and software. The ACD receives calls coming into the service center and then distributes them to the next available agent. If all agents are busy, the caller is placed in a queue. The ACD monitors the agents, and when one becomes available, routes the person that has been in the queue the longest to that agent. The system can play one or more recorded messages for customers who are in the queue. The other basic function of the ACD is to gather metrics about each of the calls and summary information about all of the calls. The system tracks the call length, total number of calls, average call length, number of calls abandoned, number of calls sent to each queue, number of calls handled by each agent, hold time, blockage, and other information.

In addition to these basic features, some ACD systems are equipped with very sophisticated capabilities, some or all of which you may find useful.

- ACDs are sophisticated enough to tell the caller how long they may have to wait until they are put through to an agent.
- ACDs can be programmed to take different actions at different times of the day or during different load levels.
- ACDs allow you to create and use multiple queues. The customer can reach the correct queue by pressing or saying a number that corresponds to a list of options they hear in a recorded message. At that point, they are either routed to a queue or they hear a message with another set of options to select from.
- ACDs allow you to route calls to multiple service centers in a distributed environment and even distribute the ACD system itself.
- ACDs allow you to use remote agents, those working from home, for example. The transaction (connecting the customer and the agent) is transparent to both the customer and the agent.
- ACDs allow you to have agents in multiple queues, so you can more easily manage overflow and better utilize your agents.
- ACD systems allow you to use skill-based routing. The purpose of skill-based routing is to offer the call to the agent who can best handle that caller. A secondary purpose of skill-based routing is to keep the agents at maximum productivity. In ACD systems, a good skill-based routing setup incorporates individual skills, as well as priorities, in assigning tickets to an agent.
- ACDs allow you to place a call in multiple queues.
- ACDs can be programmed so that, based on predetermined conditions, calls can be distributed more effectively.
- ACD systems have their own built-in reporting systems and some allow a manager to view the data online, in real-time.

While it is not a capability of the ACD system, it is important to note that some ACDs interface with workforce management software. These two systems together provide you a powerful tool for planning and optimizing your resources.

An ACD system is an extremely valuable tool. Not only does it automatically manage your calls, it also provides you with extremely valuable information that you may not be able to gather otherwise. Without call metrics, you will not be able to measure the performance of much of what your service center does. If you can't measure performance, you can't manage performance, and you will be at risk if you attempt to implement SLAs with your customers. If you have more than 40 calls a day, you should consider an ACD, if for no other reason than to capture metrics.

11.1.2 Internet

Access to the service center via any network, whether it is through the Internet or an intranet, is a very powerful tool for both the service center and the customer. I'll refer to this access generically as network access. When a customer uses the network to access the service center, they generally fill out an online form that you have developed specifically for this purpose. Depending on the level of sophistication you want to implement, you could have multiple forms available that are specific to the reason the customer is contacting the service center. Essentially, the customer uses the form to create his or her own ticket. You must give the customer instructions on how to complete the form, how to apply priorities if appropriate, and some indication of what to expect in terms of response from the service center. The customer completes the form, which is then turned into a ticket, and the system gives the customer the ticket number.

This access approach is very convenient for customers because they can provide the information to the service center at their leisure, any time of the day or night, without being "trapped" on the phone. This approach works best for customers when they do not have what they consider to be a high priority problem or incident. They may even be able to send screenshots and data, which makes it very easy for the customer to communicate exactly what the problem is. This is also a good access approach for the service center because it potentially reduces the number of calls to the service center and also the amount of immediate response that the service center must provide.

You can help the customer and yourself by implementing menus and dropdown lists that simplify the customer's task and provide valid data to the service center. One of the reasons this approach only potentially reduces calls is that the service center often has to make an outbound call to ask additional questions, and the potential for phone tag with the customer means that the customer may end up calling the service center several times before connecting with the technician. You can avoid this problem if your customer is willing to conduct the entire transaction via email; that is, additional information is passed back and forth between the customer and the technician via email.

There are two dramatically different approaches to implementing customer access to the service center via a network. One approach requires special software to be implemented on the client machine. The software handles the data integrity and functional connectivity to the PMS. This is a functionally rich approach, but requires you to install software on every client machine, which could drive up both your licensing and operating expenses. A second, and better, approach is to have a thin client that accesses the PMS via a Web browser. This eliminates the need for licensing software for each client and reduces operational overhead, while still providing the same functionality and data integrity.

11.1.3 Email

Email is a common approach that many service centers use to provide access to customers. The benefit to the customer is the same as with network access. The customer can provide the information to the service center at their leisure, without having to be trapped on the telephone. The benefits to the service center are the same as well. The approach reduces the number of calls and the amount of immediate response that the service center must provide. An additional advantage is that no special software is required for the client, since most already have email. Email also provides a detailed record of the incident, which can be transferred to the official ticket.

The most significant problem with this approach is that email is free-form. With the network accessapproach discussed in the previous section, you provide a form that guides the customer through the information you need to service the ticket. With the email approach, you get the information that the customer sends, which can be wholly insufficient to resolve the problem. With the network approach, you can force the customer to fill in mandatory fields and can use lists to force the customer to, for example, select the impacted product from a dropdown list, which then helps with routing the ticket to the correct pool. You can't do that with email. You can purchase or write code that will scan the email and attempt to pull information from the email, but this is obviously a hit-or-miss approach. Generally, a ticket is opened and the email content is transferred to the record. The other disadvantage is that the customer is not automatically provided with information, such as a ticket number and what action to expect next, which they do receive when they use the network access form.

One approach you can use to overcome some of these problems is to create forms and place them on the network where customers can access them, fill them out, and then attach them to the email. Of course, for this approach to work, the customers have to know that forms are available and where to find them. You can also send a follow-up questionnaire to the customer.

While email is a convenient approach for the customer, it is not for the service center. It will require some intervention on your part and will almost certainly require you to gather more information from the customer. Like the network approach, telephone tag may actually generate more calls to the service center than if the customer had simply called in the first place. If you use strictly email and don't revert to the phone, an email "conversation" can take much longer than the equivalent telephone conversation.

11.1.4 Fax

A facsimile is a possible approach that customers can use to contact the service center. This approach has the same advantages and disadvantages of the email approach.

▶ 11.2 Service Delivery Tools

Service delivery tools are intended to help the service center deliver support to customers. The tools help you to keep track of customers' requests and allow you to measure your service delivery performance.

There are tools available to help you increase the speed, accuracy, and consistency at which you provide solutions to your customers.

There are many important delivery tools to consider. The PMS, or help desk system, is the core service center system that documents and tracks all customer contacts, tickets, solutions, and so on. There are many ways to extend the functionality of this core system. By implementing one or more knowledge bases with your core management system, you can leverage the collective knowledge of your staff and experts outside of your company to quickly deliver consistent solutions to customers. Through the integration and use of an asset management system, technicians have immediate access to the customer's hardware and software profiles and configuration information, which can greatly improve the ability to resolve customer problems. Remote control tools allow agents to resolve problems without having to visit the customer's desktop, increasing your efficiency. Remote control tools also allow you to show customers how to perform certain tasks, such as mapping to a network drive, without your having to visit the site. Workforce management tools allow you to optimize the utilization of your resources, which is usually the single largest expense in a service center, to meet customer demands. Computer telephony integration allows you to save time in gathering customer information and delivering solutions to customers. Integration with defect-tracking software allows you to pass defects to a development group, keep track of status, and keep track of known bugs so that your agents don't waste time re-troubleshooting them. Integration with change management systems allows your service center to keep track of planned changes that could potentially generate calls to the service center.

11.2.1 Problem Management System

Problem management systems, or help desk systems, have four primary functions: to capture request information, to store that information in a common location, to route and escalate the request as necessary, and to store and report metrics on the entire process.

When a customer contacts the service center, the PMS maintains a record of the contact. This record, often referred to as a ticket, receives a unique identifier and contains profile information about the customer, such as name, location, department, phone number, hardware and software profiles, and the time of the contact. This information can be added manually by the agent or automatically if the PMS is interfaced with an automatic number identification (ANI) system (discussed later in this section). The agent then enters information about the reason for the call, including a description of the problem, attempted or final resolution, components involved, priority, and a status. The ticket contains all the details of the call, its current status, history, what actions have been taken and by which agent, and what actions may occur next.

Once a ticket is created, it is logged, or stored, in a central location. From that central location, tickets can be monitored from initiation to close-out. Agents can also route the ticket to another tier in the organization, or the PMS may automatically escalate the ticket, based on predefined criteria. In either of these cases, the ticket is modified to include information about the new agent who has the ticket and the actions that agent has taken. Tickets are generally routed into queues that belong to a pool of resources. The next agent available in that pool can see all of the tickets in the queue and should take the tickets in the order of priority.

Automatic escalation is based on predefined criteria, such as the assigned priority and the length of time the ticket has been open, but it can also be based on such factors as the type of call or type of equipment impacted. Escalation can be as simple as sending the ticket to a new queue, or it may require contacting a service center agent by phone or pager, setting off an alarm on an agent's system, or changing the color of the ticket to red (flagging it for highest priority). When the customer's problem has been resolved, the ticket is marked as closed. The PMS will either automatically notify the customer via email or fax, or notify the original agent or a designee so that they can contact the customer.

Queries and reports can be run against the central repository of tickets. Most PMSs contain numerous prebuilt reports that will be of great value to you in evaluating the service center's performance. Among the most useful information are the metrics about the length of time it took to close the ticket. This will allow you to verify if you are meeting the service level targets established in your SLAs. The canned reports are also very helpful for reviewing the effectiveness of your problem management processes. You can check to see if tickets are being correctly routed or if they are being routed too frequently. You can evaluate your escalation process to see if it is working as designed and if there is room for improvement. You can check to see if you are meeting your first tier resolution targets and individual agent performance for ratio of opened to closed tickets. You can also have real-time reporting against the repository that generates a report or initiates an alarm when certain conditions are met. In addition to reporting on what has already occurred, the PMS reports can show you trends with forecasts and projections. These are extremely valuable because they let you take corrective action proactively, before the problem occurs or escalates.

Another important capability of PMS is the ability for your technicians to access it from anywhere. For example, if you are an internal service center providing support to employees of your company, the PMS's remote access feature allows your technicians to retrieve and update tickets from any desktop. This is a useful feature because the technician can close the ticket on the spot rather than waiting until he or she gets back to the service center. Efficiency is improved, because the technician doesn't have to remember what work was done, the close time on the ticket better reflects the actual time, and you can begin your close-out procedures earlier. This capability also allows the technician to get the next ticket without having to return to his or her desk. An additional benefit is that if the technician gets stopped by a customer who hasn't contacted the help desk first, a new ticket can be opened and closed right from the customer's desktop. While that customer behavior is not encouraged, it happens all too frequently, and at least this approach allows you to keep track of the work that was done.

Another approach to enabling mobile agents to keep on-the-spot records is to provide dispatched agents with palm computing devices. When on a call, the agent can update the ticket or create a new one in the palm device. The palm device is synchronized with the PMS. The agent's changes are uploaded into the PMS and new tickets are downloaded to the palm device. This approach still entails delays between the time the work is completed and the time the ticket changes are uploaded into the PMS, but without this ability, the work is quite often done and no record of it is maintained, which, of course, ruins your metrics.

The PMS should be intuitive and easy to use. This reduces the amount of training for the agents who use the system. Many PMSs have the ability to document your procedures and provide that information to your agents. This will also help to reduce your training time. How the information is accessed varies by system; some systems use an online help approach, some implement procedures as workflow, and others use wizard-like cue cards that prompt agents through tasks. Once an agent is up to speed, the cue cards can be turned off.

Problem management systems have many other valuable uses beyond the basic functions listed here. By integrating with other tools and using add-on modules, the PMS can be greatly enhanced. As mentioned, it can integrate with the ACD/ANI to provide customer information to the agent just before the call comes in and to populate the ticket. It can also be integrated with an SLA module to create and track metrics against the online SLA. Other good candidates for integration include knowledge base, workforce management, asset management, configuration management, defect tracking, Internet, service provisioning, email, fax, and IVR systems. All of these add-ons are discussed in the following sections.

11.2.2 Online SLA

Some PMSs today have a module available that will allow you to build your SLA right into the system and then report back against it. The system must let you document all of your commitments and the metrics used to measure your performance, and must have built-in reports that track your actual performance against the commitments. This is an extremely useful feature because it makes the monitoring of your performance against the SLA very simple, at least as compared to the traditional SLA, which is gathering dust somewhere in a three-ring binder. A comprehensive online module will also send alerts that notify you when service level commitments are at risk and will allow you to implement automatic escalation procedures. An additional feature to look for is the ability to automatically schedule, run, and distribute reports. This can reduce your reporting overhead.

Vendors implement online SLAs differently. The online SLA can be as simple as a text document that identifies key service metrics and then gathers actual performance metrics. A more sophisticated strategy is to build the SLA based on a service catalog. Services and specific commitments against those services are added to the SLA, and then actual performance is gathered to compare against the commitment.

11.2.3 Computer Telephone Integration

Computer telephone integration (CTI) is a strategy, not a specific type of tool. The strategy is to interface, or integrate, the telephone system with other computer systems you use in the service center. The purposes are to provide better service to your customers, reduce call length, and reduce customer/agent interaction. CTI can be used to personalize your transactions and relationships with your customers. This can create customer loyalty and repeat business, because customers generally prefer to do business with service centers that "know" them and know how to satisfy their needs. Integrated voice response and automatic number identification systems are examples of the CTI strategy.

11.2.4 Automatic Number Identification

ANI is part of the CTI strategy. In locations where ANI is available, the service center can use a caller's phone number for various purposes. The most common usage is to retrieve information about the customer (using the phone number) and route that information to the agent just prior to the agent taking the call. This saves the agent from having to look up information about the caller and can shave seconds off of the total length of the call. Over the course of a year, those seconds can add up to significant time savings and therefore significant dollar savings. The more calls you receive, the more you save.

The downside to ANI is that callers don't always call from the same phone. To overcome this limitation, companies may design an application into their CTI implementation that will allow them to automatically update the ANI customer database with the new number. In this scenario, the system adds the new number to the database without any participation from the agent or the customer. The other automated alternative lets the agent verify that this is a valid number for the customer prior to adding the new number to the database.

If ANI is not available, or if the number the customer is calling from does not match any number in the database, the customer may be prompted to enter some other number, such as a customer ID, employee number, home phone number, or PIN number. One important thing to keep in mind if you're going to use this approach is that you must verify that the caller and the person that the system found are one and the same.

11.2.5 Workforce Management Software

There are numerous workforce management systems available on the market. The most useful to you depends on the size and complexity of your operation and the types of tools you currently use. This software allows you to optimize resource schedules, based on information from your ACD system. Many of these systems will directly interface to your ACD. The more sophisticated of these systems will also help you optimize scheduling based on agent skills. Some systems help optimize scheduling across multiple sites and will work in near real-time to help you make changes on the fly as necessary.

Keep in mind that even a slight improvement in utilization can save you significant dollars, because your agents are generally your biggest expense.

11.2.6 Remote Control Software

Remote control software provides the service center agent with the ability to take control of a customer's PC directly from the agent's PC. The agent can view a customer's screen and take over the keyboard and mouse to operate the customer's PC as if he or she were sitting at the customer's desk. This technology allows the service center to provide "onsite" support without having to incur the cost of traveling to the site. This type of remote support can be used for any customer node on the network, as well as for dial-up connections (although not as effectively).

Remote control technology has many benefits for the service center. It allows the service center agent to gather information that the customer would normally have to provide over the phone or that the agent would have to find by visiting the customer's desktop. The technology allows the service center agent to show the customer what to do instead of explaining it over the phone or via email. The customer can sit back and watch the agent's keystrokes and mouse clicks while the agent tells the customer what he or she is doing.

The use of remote control software can significantly reduce service center costs by reducing the frequency of agent dispatching. The travel-time savings alone allows each agent to handle more requests.

The use of remote control technology often faces resistance that can reduce its effectiveness. The resistance comes from customers who are concerned about their privacy and from technicians who would rather go out and visit the customer's desktop. These are not trivial issues, but they can be overcome. The customers' concern can be addressed by giving them the option to allow or not allow the agent to take control. It is more difficult to resolve the technicians' resistance because it is a cultural issue. If you're implementing remote control in this environment, tight managerial control will be required until the culture is changed. The manager will have to have a thorough understanding of the capabilities of the tool to distinguish between what it can do and what the technicians claim it can't do.

Another consideration prior to implementing remote control is who—which tier or group—will use the technology. The simplest approach is to provide the tools to any group that would normally be dispatched to provide desktop software support. However, some service centers are providing the tools to each agent in tier 1 to improve first-touch resolution and reduce the number of tickets routed and escalated to subsequent tiers. This is an extremely effective approach, but it is not the right solution for all service centers. As the computing environments you support become more complex, you may find that the number of calls you can resolve during the initial contact is dropping. If this is the situation, you may find that your tier 1 support is transitioning from a group that resolves problems to a group that dispatches (routes or escalates) problems. Your costs will begin to increase and your resolution times will fall. If you are in this situation, you may want to consider implementing remote control for tier 1 agents. This approach will require that tier 1 agents spend more time resolving each problem, but your overall resolution time will decrease because you save time by not routing and escalating calls to subsequent tiers. The key to making the decision of implementing the tools at tier 1 versus some subsequent tier depends on the volume and type of calls that are being escalated that could be resolved at tier 1 with remote control tools. It is also important to consider that more resources may be required at tier 1, because agents will be solving problems that they had been dispatching and may be spending more time on each call.

One final note: Look for remote control tools that you can tightly integrate with your PMS. This will save your agents time because they will not have to do so much "jumping" between applications, and it can limit redundant data entry. You may want to consider purchasing a desktop management system that includes remote control capability. DMS capabilities are discussed later in this chapter.

11.2.7 Asset Management

Asset management systems document all hardware and software that the service center supports. Some asset management systems can also capture all costs related to each asset and give you a consolidated financial view of your environment. Most systems have automated agents that search the network and automatically gather and store the information. Most systems also allow you to document information about equipment that is not connected to the network, such as laptops and palm computing devices. You can set the agents up so that when a laptop dials in, the agent grabs the information required for the database before the laptop disconnects. If it doesn't get all of the information during the session, it can pick up where it left off during the next section. Additional capabilities include license management, financial tracking, and warranty tracking. The auto-discovery agents can be scheduled to run during off hours so that they do not impact customers and can continually keep the asset database up to date with accurate information. Some systems have the ability to remove software as well, such as software that is not standard for your environment.

An interface between the PMS and the asset management system provides the service center with valuable detailed and accurate information about the customers' environment. That data can greatly reduce the agents' troubleshooting time. The ability to remove software can also reduce your calls, by automatically removing nonstandard software that could create problems.

11.2.8 Change Management

Change management systems automate change control processes. Change control processes do as the name implies. The processes are in place to ensure that changes to the production environment occur in a controlled fashion, by analyzing and managing the impact and risks. Any proposed changes, such as hardware, software, or standard configuration, is documented and tracked in the change control, or change management system. The control is exercised by one or more people (sometimes a change control board) who are responsible for reviewing and approving what will be done, making sure all the proper testing and related tasks are performed (or are planned), and establishing a proactive communication plan to notify anyone who may be affected.

Proactively notifying customers that something is being done can reduce the number of calls to the service center. For example, if a server is going to be down for maintenance, customers can be notified in advance so that they do not call the service center to report the outage as a problem. Comprehensive change management systems have complete scheduling and resource assignment capabilities, provide a workflow component to automate approval and notification functions, and have both canned and ad hoc reporting capabilities.

Good change control processes also make sure that the service center is notified and receives training prior to releasing something new or modified into the customer environment. Obviously, being trained in advance is critical for the service center to provide adequate support Often, someone from the service center participates as a member of the change control board, ensuring that the service center is proactively prepared for changes that may impact customers.

Customers often call to request new or enhanced functionality, or they call to report a bug that is really an enhancement request. What do you normally do with that information? With an interface to a change management system, you can document those requests to make sure they don't fall through the cracks, and that may reduce call volume for you in the future. You could also initiate change requests on your own that would help eliminate problem areas in the customer environment. Again, this can help you reduce call volume.

The benefits to the service center of interfacing with a change management system are that the interface gives you valuable information and provides a place to document customer enhancement requests.

11.2.9 Defect Tracking

Defect-tracking systems are typically used by software development teams to track bugs. The system captures important information about bugs, such as the steps to recreate the bug, the product affected, the module affected, the code version affected, the environment where the problem occurs, the status of the bug, the person or team working on it, when it should be fixed, and a link to the replacement code. If you can interface your PMS with the defect-tracking system, the service center can access and share valuable data. For example, via the interface, you could upload known bugs into your knowledge base. If you don't have a knowledge base, you could use the defect-tracking system as a knowledge base (if your interface gives you that type of access). This is handy if a customer encounters a problem with an in-house-developed product, because you could access information about the product and specific module in your knowledge base or get even more information from the defect-tracking tool. With direct access, you could inform the customer of the status and plan for the defect.

Another benefit is that if you discover a new bug with in-house software, you could enter it directly into the development team's defect management tool. This ensures that bugs do not fall through the cracks. Further, this approach allows the development team to use their own tools instead of forcing them to also use your problem management software.

11.2.10 Knowledge Base Software

Knowledge bases are extremely powerful tools that can significantly improve your ability to deliver services to your customer base. A knowledge base contains solutions and workarounds to known problems and allows your agents to access those solutions to resolve customer problems. Knowledge bases provide many potential benefits to the service center. When properly implemented, a knowledge base documents the collective knowledge of your service center agents and leverages that knowledge by making it available to all agents. This ability alone overcomes a common problem in many service centers: communicating solutions to everyone who needs them. In addition to your internal knowledge, product-specific and third-party multiproduct knowledge base content is available for purchase so that you can leverage external knowledge as well.

When properly implemented and used, the knowledge base stops agents from redundantly troubleshooting problems. The knowledge base documents problems and symptoms as well as solutions and workarounds. Typically, an agent receives a call and if he or she does not know the solution, they generally begin troubleshooting or analyzing the problem, and then move on to identifying a solution. If a knowledge base is available, the process is slightly different. The agent receives a problem and if he or she does not know the solution, the next step is to check the knowledge base, not start troubleshooting.

Without the knowledge base, the agent thinks, "I'm not familiar with the problem. Let's figure out what's causing it and how to fix it." With a knowledge base, the agent thinks, "I'm not familiar with the problem. Let's see if anyone else has encountered it, and if so, what they did to resolve it."

Another significant benefit of knowledge bases is that if agents use it properly, they can consistently apply solutions and workarounds. Consistency reduces support costs because it reduces "one-offs" (custom solutions). If new solutions or better workarounds become available, they too can be consistently applied.

There are different types of knowledge bases, but one fact that is consistent across them all is that the information that comes out is only as good as what goes in. The old adage "garbage in, garbage out" certainly holds true with knowledge bases, so if you are going to implement one, you must be prepared to deal with the overhead required to make sure that what goes in is good. You certainly do not want to propagate bad solutions or workarounds. Someone will have to validate knowledge base reports prior to releasing them into the knowledge base. You also have to make sure that they are consistently formatted and well written for ease of use and understanding. Finally, to be effective, every common problem and solution must be captured, documented, and updated as necessary. These three tasks, gathering, documenting, and testing, represent a significant amount of work and cannot be overlooked or underestimated if you want to implement a knowledge base that will actually be used.

Another important consideration is training for agents. It is a fact that given a good knowledge base, the agent who is best at finding and retrieving the information will be more productive and successful at resolving customer problems than other agents, regardless of their technical knowledge.

As mentioned previously, there are different types of knowledge bases. The primary difference is based on how information is retrieved and thus how it is stored. The most common knowledge bases are document- or text-based storage and retrieval systems. In this model, a standard document is used to document a single problem and solution, and all the known symptoms. It is important that these documents all use the same format. A text retrieval engine searches the database for the keywords entered by the service center agent, which makes the system simple to use. The benefits of this approach is that it is easy to design and to add, update, and remove knowledge base documents as necessary. The potential problems occur as the database grows in size. A search may return hundreds or thousands of documents that match the agent's search criteria. The agent must then look through these to find the correct document, which can dramatically increase the time it takes to resolve the issue. This could cause agents to avoid using the system, thus eliminating the benefits of having a knowledge base.

The other type of knowledge base system uses expert-based knowledge to lead the agent to the correct information. Generally, the knowledge base information is organized or accessed hierarchically. The knowledge base retrieval model attempts to simulate the troubleshooting approach. The agent selects from a list of choices and/or questions to navigate through the hierarchy until he or she reaches the desired information. For example, the agent may start by selecting a product or type of product (Microsoft PowerPoint or network printer) at the highest level of the hierarchy. Based on that choice, a new set of options is presented, which, upon selection, navigate deeper into the hierarchy. For example, if the agent chose network printer at the highest level of the hierarchy, the next level may present a list of network printers to choose from. Or, if the agent selected Microsoft PowerPoint at one level of the hierarchy, the next level may ask the agent what type of Microsoft PowerPoint problem he or she is having and present a list of the most common problems. The agent selects the problem and continues navigating deeper into the hierarchy. This is a good approach for agents, because they do not require much training to use it effectively. The downside to this approach is that it requires much more design planning on the part of the service center. It also requires significant maintenance to provide the right options for navigating the hierarchy and accessing new solutions. As the customer environment being supported becomes more complex, so does the hierarchy required to support it. This approach works best for common and well-known problems.

Variations of the hierarchic approach are often referred to as case-based systems, decision tree systems, and troubleshooting systems. They all use a hierarchy but use different selection criteria to navigate the hierarchy or decision tree. A fourth variation of this approach uses a network structure rather than a hierarchy. The benefit is that an agent can navigate through the data rather than up and down the hierarchy; thus if the information is not found, the agent doesn't have to back all the way out and start over. An additional benefit is that because the system uses a network architecture, it is easier to add new information, because there is no rigid hierarchic structure to redesign. The downside to this approach is that because of the tool's inherent flexibility, more process rigidity must be implemented by the organization to ensure that the data does not get out of control.

11.2.11 Email

As an access tool, email has some disadvantages, mentioned previously. As a service delivery tool, email has advantages for the service center. Email makes it simple to prioritize incoming requests because there is no need for immediate response. Once prioritized, the problem can be handled in a more appropriate fashion than is available with incoming phone calls, which are processed on a first come, first served basis. This helps you reduce your immediate response staffing needs and also allows you to spread requests out and improve agent utilization rates.

Another benefit is that an agent can attach detailed instructions for the customer to follow rather than stepping the customer through the instructions over the phone. This is especially efficient if you have a knowledge base and the problem and solution are already documented in the system. The agent merely has to locate the correct document and attach it to the email he or she is returning to the customer. An alternative to using an attachment is to include a URL in the email that points to the appropriate knowledge base document. Email also generates a written record of the entire transaction, which can be copied into the ticket. If it is a new problem not already documented in the knowledge base, the solution the agent discovers and sends to the customer can be used as the basis of a new knowledge base document.

An additional benefit is the use of email to "push" information to the customer base. This allows the service center to proactively support the customers and eliminate calls. Suppose, for example, that a recurring problem has been resolved or a workaround has been identified. The service center can email the solution to customers and thus eliminate future calls.

11.2.12 Fax

Assuming you send and receive faxes as electronic documents, the fax has the same advantages and disadvantages as a service delivery tool as email.

11.2.13 Internet

A service center that has access to the Internet has a wealth of information available to aid it in servicing customers. Service center agents can research problems via the Internet and have access to incredible volumes of product information. Agents can access a vendor's Web site and often, the vendor's knowledge base, to find solutions, patches, downloads, and other helpful information that will benefit the service center. The agent can then transmit the solution to all of his or her customers who need it. An agent can post questions in worldwide discussion groups and get help from others who have already experienced the problem. Agents can also network with their peers in other support organizations to share incredible amounts of valuable information. The information available over the World Wide Web is amazing, and every service center, no matter how small or large, should take advantage of it.

If your service center is network-enabled and you have a Web page or maintain list servers, you can ask customers to complete online surveys. The results are valuable metrics about your performance and your customers' desires. A network-enabled service center can also deploy remote agents that can do anything that a local agent can do. If your company is promoting telecommuting, network-enabling is a must. The use of remote agents also allows you to successfully utilize part-time resources for peak shaving. This is attractive for both the part-time resources and the service center. Part-timers do not have to commute and can work from home, and the service center does not have to provide desk space, parking, and other on-site accommodations that add to the center's overhead.

The Internet provides so much capability that policies and procedures governing its use are required. You need to make sure that agents who use the Internet understand licensing and distribution issues. You need to develop policies and make sure agents understand and follow them as well. Firewalls, encryption, and virus protection strategies must be implemented to protect your company and make sure you do not create your own support nightmares.

▶ 11.3 Proactive Monitoring Tools

Proactive monitoring tools are tools that have the ability to monitor your environment and warn you before something in the environment fails. With properly implemented and integrated monitoring tools, you can drastically reduce your service center costs by eliminating problems that would generate calls before they happen. This also reduces customer downtime. These two benefits together can significantly reduce your company's total cost of ownership for information technology.

Monitoring is only one capability of these tool sets. Most also have remote control, software distribution, reboot, execute, and hardware and software inventorying capabilities tightly integrated. Inventory (asset management) and remote control have already been discussed, so this section will focus on monitoring capabilities and benefits.

You tell the tools what you want to monitor and then establish alert thresholds. For example, you may set a threshold of 80 percent for hard drive utilization in one of your customer's key desktop machines. The monitoring software has an agent that watches the utilization for that desktop machine. When the agent sees the drive utilization cross the threshold, it sends an alert to the monitoring station. If your PMS is integrated with the monitoring tool, you can automatically generate a ticket to upgrade the machine before the customer calls with a real hard drive-related problem. Think about the savings. With or without the monitoring tools, the system had to be upgraded, so those costs are the same. By doing the upgrade proactively, though, the customer didn't have any problem-related downtime, the service center didn't receive a call, and an agent didn't have to spend time troubleshooting. Suppose you set a memory utilization threshold of 80 percent in one of your key servers. A monitoring agent sits out there and monitors the server. When the threshold is crossed, the agent sends an alert. Because it is a production server, you can generate a ticket, interface with the change management system, and initiate a managed project to upgrade the server memory. Imagine the number of calls diverted and the amount of customer downtime avoided by upgrading the system before the server failed. Further, you saved money because you didn't have to scramble a team to troubleshoot and resolve a priority 1 incident. These are very simple examples, but they illustrate the power and value of the technology.

It is important to note that these systems can generate an enormous number of alerts. The server may cross the 80 percent memory utilization alert threshold 50 times in a day. Different systems handle warnings and alerts in different ways, but the key for you to consider is that you want to generate only one ticket based on the alert. Since, in this example, you have already initiated a project to upgrade it, you don't want another ticket generated. Further, you probably don't want to hear about it again unless it crosses, say, a 90 percent threshold before it is fixed. At that point, you want to escalate the problem. Check with the vendor to find out how the system can provide you with the correct data.

Another consideration is that a problem in one place may cause many other related problems, all of which generate alerts. When this occurs, you want a ticket that addresses the real problem and not a ticket for each symptom or related problem. For example, suppose a router goes down and generates an alert. It is also likely that many other components that attempt to use that router will generate their own alerts, indicating that they are having a problem. One problem in a key location can cause a ripple of cascading alerts. To handle this situation, vendors and third-party add-ins provide event correlation software to filter the cascading alerts.

A complete discussion of these complex but highly valuable tools is beyond the scope of this book, but there are several key considerations that require mentioning. It is unrealistic to expect that you can find one tool that can provide management services (thresholds, monitoring, simulation, performance management, software distribution, probes, agents, and so on) across your entire IT infrastructure. A single vendor's software can cover a significant portion of the infrastructure, but not all of it. Therefore, it is important to choose a vendor and tool that allows for third-party add-ins to provide services for specific components. The primary tool provides the backbone management and monitoring tool, and incorporates the third-party add-ins to the backbone. This will prevent you from having to set up multiple monitoring stations.

These are complex tools, so you should not believe that you can buy it, install it, and be off and running in a day or two. Budget for a lot of training and implementation support. If you don't, you may find yourself using 10 percent of the system's capabilities and overwhelming yourself with alerts in one area, while not gathering enough data from other areas.

Do not plan to automatically generate tickets as soon as the network or desktop management software is installed. Leave time to fine-tune the implementation of the tools, specifically the threshold monitoring. It takes time to get these tuned to generate the appropriate warnings and alerts.

▶ 11.4 Customer-Enabling Tools

Customer-enabling tools are both access tools and service delivery tools. The use of these tools allows customers to get the information they need without the intervention of the service center staff. Obviously, the more customers you can get to find their own solutions, the fewer requests you have to service, thus eliminating calls and other requests that require your staff. Enabling tools can dramatically reduce your service costs, and if well-implemented, can improve customer satisfaction. Enabling tools are available 24/7 and can therefore improve your ability to deliver support during nonstandard working hours.

11.4.1 Integrated Voice Response

The purpose of the IVR is to identify the need of the customer and then take some action, based on the customer's input, without having to have an agent involved. The IVR capability is based, to some extent, on what the IVR is integrated with. The customer enters a selection over the phone, based on a menu, and the IVR takes some action. The IVR is a good application for handling simple, redundant requests. The IVR can play prerecorded answers to common questions, provide status information, send a fax, reset printers, reboot equipment, and more, depending on what the IVR is integrated with. The IVR can also pass the customer requirement to the ACD so that the ACD can then distribute the call using skill-set routing. This requires an intelligent link between the IVR and the ACD. Suppose, for example, that you receive numerous calls on a daily basis about how to upload information from a palm computing device to a PC. The customer can use a menu in the IVR to navigate to prerecorded messages with instructions or can have that information faxed or emailed. An agent never has to get involved. If you receive numerous simple, redundant calls of this nature, this technology can greatly reduce the number of calls your agents need to process. You should consider IVR as an agent to handle all of your frequently asked questions (FAQs) and even notify customers if patches or downloads are available and how to get them. You can also use IVR to post alert information. For example, if a server is down, you can post that information on the IVR system and therefore eliminate calls from customers. An additional benefit of IVR is that it allows your customers to get support 24 hours a day, 7 days a week.

One of IVR's biggest benefits is that once it is set up, it requires very little manual intervention. That can also be one of its biggest downfalls, if you're not careful. IVRs can take care of thousands of customer calls without any manual intervention and generally handle it very well. As a result, they are often set up and then forgotten. The IVR is integrated to many other systems, though, that can impact the IVR performance. The IVR can be connected to multiple database servers and networks. Performance degradation to any of those devices could negatively impact IVR performance. Changes to any of those devices can inadvertently impact the IVR, and you may never know it happened. Suppose, for example, that the IVR is linked to a database that, for whatever reason, slows down dramatically. The IVR customers trying to retrieve data from that server will zero out to the service center. Suddenly, service center calls spike with callers zeroing out of the IVR. Even worse, customers may simply hang up and you would have no indication that something was wrong. The bottom line is that you must monitor IVR performance.

11.4.2 Internet

Network enabling the service center has many of the same benefits as IVR in terms of allowing customers to serve themselves. You can create a Web page as a gateway to the service center, which customers can access via a local or wide area network or via the Internet. The Web page gives customers access to service center tools, allowing them to help themselves without requiring intervention of service center agents.

A good service center Web page can help you to reduce your costs by making your customers self-sufficient and by allowing you to provide solutions proactively. You can give your customers access to all or some controlled portion of your knowledge base. If you use a text-based knowledge base, your customers can use text-based search engines to locate knowledge base documents to resolve their problems. A hierarchic knowledge base may be even more useful for customers, because it can guide the customer, just as your agents do, through the process of locating the information they need. Hierarchic knowledge bases are best suited for use with frequently occurring problems.

Like the IVR, the Web page is a good place to post a list of FAQs and answers. Keep the link to your FAQs in a prominent location so that it is easy for your customers to find. Keep the list as short as possible, or customers may not use it and will opt instead to use the knowledge base search engine. You should also post alerts, or at least a link to alerts, on the main page. This can really help to reduce calls about incidents that impact a large number of customers.

The Web page is a good place to post information about available upgrades and patches. Even if you use a software distribution system to automatically upgrade your customer base, chances are that you have some remote customers that you cannot reach via your software distribution system. The Web page can provide those customers access to the upgrades. While your service center Web site is a natural choice to provide upgrades, it may not be the best solution, depending on your needs. If you want to force standardization on remote machines, you should consider other tools. Tools are available that specialize in pushing software to remote machines and also allow for remote control and asset inventory of remote machines. These tools have two significant advantages over the Web. First, they can force the upgrade and thus keep remote users up to standards. Second, they have checkpoint-resume capability in case of accidental disconnects, which is critical for large transfers over slow dial-up lines.

An additional benefit of network enabling your service center is that you can distribute (push) important information to your customers. Depending on the types of lists you maintain, you can do both mass and targeted distributions.

If your service center is responsible for all contact with customers (support, service, sales, information, and so on), a Web page is an absolute requirement. This approach is commonly referred to as customer resource management (CRM), and the service center provides cradle-to-grave support for the customers. If this describes your service center, then you obviously need to organize your main Web page so that customers are directed to the information they need. This can include pages for checking order status, placing orders, accessing account information, making payments, troubleshooting problems, and more.

Network enabling your service center also provides you with the opportunity to provide customer support via news and chat groups. The use of newsgroups and chat sessions can reduce the number of calls to the support center. Many large companies use topical-focused chat rooms and newsgroups as forum for customers to post questions. The service center can respond with answers and solutions for all interested customers to see and can make an archive of the questions and answers available for customers to review. Even better, expert users who are not part of the service center will often take the time to provide answers, saving the service center from doing the work. One potential concern is that someone may provide inaccurate information, which can then be propagated among the online community, so it is definitely worth the effort to monitor the activities.

If you plan to implement a Web gateway, you need to consider how you will deploy it. You can deploy it starting with limited functionality to a large customer group, or you can deploy a fully functional Web page to a small pilot group. Both are good approaches. If you implement to a large customer base, start with limited functionality and then incrementally add new functionality. This controlled approach allows you to manage growth and to market the Web access internally. If you decide to roll out a fully functional Web page, you should consider rolling it out to a pilot group first. This will allow you to solicit and incorporate customer feedback prior to giving access to the entire customer base. This will also allow you to manage growth andeinsure adequate performance. You can also begin a marketing campaign while you're fine-tuning the systems. Once the kinks are worked out, continue adding new customer groups incrementally.

From the marketing perspective, give your customers an incentive to use the new system and become more self-enabled. Offer them something like coffee mugs or pens, or set up a raffle. Airlines offer discounts and additional frequent flyer miles to entice customers to use their systems for the same reason: It reduces resource requirements and saves them money. You could offer preferred service levels for Web access during the first year. The key is to create awareness and give customers an incentive.

Motivation

World-class processes and the best tools available will not make your service center the best of class and may not increase your customers' level of satisfaction. Processes and tools are simply enablers that give you and your service center staff the opportunity to satisfy your customers. Taking advantage of those opportunities—or not—is a choice that each and every member of the service center staff makes, all day long.

Making the choice to do everything possible to help the customer is solely dependent on the individual's motivation to do so. Two highly skilled carpenters with the same skill levels and the same tools can produce radically different results on the same project, depending on their motivation and enthusiasm.

People have good days and bad days, so even if you provide a magnificent work environment in which everyone is motivated and pulls together to achieve goals, there will be days when some people just don't perform up to their standards. You have to expect it of your peers, your team, and yourself.

There are many different techniques you can and should use to keep your team motivated. Some techniques are more expensive than others, so be sure to choose techniques that you can apply consistently.

▶ 12.1 Motivation Through Reward

To motivate a person, you have to understand that individual's needs. What inspires you may or may not inspire someone else. This fact, which seems so obvious, is often overlooked. Money is the classic example. In every place that I have ever worked, the assumption has been that if you want people to work harder, offer them more money, and to keep them working hard, reward their hard work with a bonus (positive reinforcement). I have always believed this to be the case, because it works for me, but money is only one way to motivate your employees.

Managers have often found themselves puzzled when offering money results little, if any, effect on some people. If you take a moment to think about it, it may become obvious why this technique often fails. The technique works or fails on different people because people work for different reasons. Recognizing these reasons is important in knowing your employees and understanding how to motivate them. Work habits often reflect what is important to and what motivates a person.

People typically referred to as hard-chargers are those who work very hard and go the extra mile, usually without prompting. They understand the goals and objectives and are willing to do whatever it takes to get the job done. Some hard-chargers really care about achieving the goals, while others care more about getting recognition and promotion. Money is typically a good motivator for hard-chargers, whether they are motivated by goals or recognition. In either case, though, money will only go so far. At some point, it will no longer motivate them to work harder. Money in and of itself is even less effective in motivating people who work because they have to or simply for something to do.

What is really at issue are needs and satisfaction. Everyone has needs and has defined (either consciously or not) levels at which those needs will be satisfied. When those needs are satisfied, there is less internal drive to focus efforts on meeting those needs. Conversely, when focusing effort to satisfy one need reduces far enough the satisfaction of another need, the effort will be stopped. This is exactly what occurs when money is used as a motivator. For the hard-chargers, if they do not reach their satisfaction level in terms of income, the enormous and continuous effort they put forward detracts from their other needs outside of work. When the hard-charger reaches an internal threshold such that the amount of work they are providing detracts too much from other important things in their lives, no amount of money can get more from them. When an employee reaches that internal threshold, you should probably not consider upping the ante, because if they did go for it, it is possible that they will "burn out."

Money is not the only reward that can motivate employees. From the perspective of rewarding someone for hard work, money is nice, but is also impersonal. You could possibly strengthen your relationship with an employee and truly make an employee feel appreciated by rewarding him or her with a more personal gift. Obviously, do not confuse personal with intimate, or you will be in real trouble. However, let's say an employee really goes the extra mile and you would like to reward him or her, but you want to do something a little more personal than money and you don't want to spend a fortune. There are many things you can do that would be very much appreciated, would not be expensive, but would require that you know something about the employee. For example, suppose a junior technician worked three weekends in a row to help out. Further, suppose you know that the employee enjoys rock climbing. A perfect and personal reward may be to buy climbing rope and give it to the employee as a thank you for the extra effort. The employee feels good that her extra effort was recognized and appreciated, and also that you know something about her and that you put some thought into the reward. You have to exercise common sense when rewarding with a personal gift, so that it doesn't backfire on you, but it can really make an employee feel appreciated and motivated. Another example is a new employee who recently relocated to work for the company. His parents were planning to visit him two weeks before a major deliverable was due. He did the right thing, from the company's perspective, and canceled their visit because he was going to be too busy to spend time with them. After the job was done, the company bought tickets for his parents to come and visit him. Not only was the employee thrilled, so were his parents. They all thought very highly of the company that would do that for an employee. From that point forward, you could always count on him in a pinch. He also always encouraged those around him. Another example is the employee who spent a lot of personal time to create some very nice graphics for the company Web page. When it was discovered that the employee's son helped, in this case did a lot of the work, the business unit president wrote a thank you letter that the employee's son could use as resume collateral in the future, when he graduated from college. The business unit president asked the employee to bring his son in to the office, where he presented him with the letter and personally thanked him. It took no more than 10 minutes of the president's time, but the employee and his entire family were extremely appreciative, because it was all unexpected. It went much farther and meant much more to the employee than money. Obviously, not all companies will allow you to give your employees these kinds of rewards. The point is to know what is happening in your employees' lives and what is important to them, and then be creative.

12.1.1 Recognition and Praise

Recognition and praise are often overlooked as reward, which is unfortunate, since they can be every bit as powerful as any other type of reward. For many people, this is far more important than a monetary reward. Generally, everyone seeks some form of recognition and praise for their work. The level of importance varies from person to person, so to successfully use this technique, you must know your employees.

Recognition and praise can come in many forms, from public accolades at a banquet to a personal handshake and thank you. Again, which is most appropriate depends to a large extent on the employee being recognized. Some employees may be shy and prefer low profile recognition, while others want to see their name in the company newsletter and receive their handshake on stage in front of all their peers.

Always put recognition and praise in writing. The employee or team being recognized should have something to show off and be proud of. Besides, seeing it will continue to inspire them in the future and remind them of what they did to earn it. Recognition reinforces the positive behavior you want to encourage and helps people and teams build positive self-images.

If you plan to use praise and recognition as a motivator, and you should, use it wisely. Make sure you provide special recognition and praise only when an employee or a team has achieved something worthy of special notice. If you overuse it or provide it when someone does only what is expected of them, the technique rapidly loses effectiveness because no one buys in.

One exception to consider is that if you are counseling an employee or team that has been underperforming, you should recognize them when they achieve the expected performance level (positive reinforcement). It may be best to provide this recognition privately, though, unless you want to publicly recognize a group as the "most improved." This approach may be appropriate with a team, but is probably not appropriate for an individual.

Recognition and praise is a very valuable tool, but it does mean that people and teams have to have the opportunity to do something above and beyond what is expected of them. Consider giving employees and teams assignments that are out of the norm so they have a chance to exceed expectations. For example, you could challenge each tier 1 team to modify their work processes to improve their performance. If they do, recognize them. That assignment includes two other powerful motivators: empowerment and challenge.

Rewards, as the proverbial carrot or an unexpected reward after the fact, are very effective motivators. However, in and of themselves, they will only work to a point. If you are understaffed and expect employees to constantly work extra hours or beyond "normal" expectations, rewards will lose their effectiveness.

▶ 12.2 Motivation Through Incentives

Many companies use formalized incentives as a motivator. It is a typical sales or piecework model. Sell or make x number of units and here is your reward. This is a very effective technique and volumes of materials have been written on the subject, so we will not spend a lot of time on it here. One key point is to make sure you set the incentive targets carefully and correctly, because they could turn against you. Suppose, for example, that you establish tier 1 closure rate targets with incentives. Consider what employees may do to achieve those rates. If an agent sacrifices quality documentation or common courtesy with the customer to reach the target rate, you probably haven't successfully achieved your ultimate goal. Further, you must make sure checks and balances are in place so the system isn't abused, or so that employees don't game the system, as in the much-publicized futures trading business.

Other incentives often used include stock options, profit sharing, and perks such as paid parking, expense accounts, subsidies, day care, transportation, telecommuting, tuition, and training. Generally, for these incentives, the company has to establish programs on a company-wide basis, and the programs will usually be out of your control. If they don't exist, they are much more complex to implement than a simple after-the-fact reward. If your company does not have such programs, then you should certainly encourage the company to develop them, because many of your competitors do. These kinds of programs are very effective for attracting staff and, if the company is successful, can be very effective in motivating the staff to do whatever is possible to help the company.

▶ 12.3 Other Motivation Techniques

There are many techniques other than incentive and reward that can be used to motivate employees and teams. These include providing opportunity, empowerment, and challenge.

12.3.1 Opportunity

For many people, opportunity is a key motivator. Opportunity to grow professionally is very important, as most people do not want to be in a "dead-end" job. Career advancement is an important tool for motivation. Providing your staff with the opportunity for promotion can be highly effective in keeping them motivated. Not only does it allow them to receive more money (in most cases), but it also provides them with recognition. It recognizes the fact that they have mastered the previous level and have earned the right to move up to the next level.

If possible, companies should try to provide both a management and a technical track. Some employees will want the opportunity to be managers, while others will not. If you do not have a technical track, you run the risk of losing your technical expertise when they reach the top level of their current track and they do not want to become managers.

The U.S. General Accounting Office conducted a review of the federal government's ability to attract and retain high-quality technical resources. Many agencies had difficulty retaining their technical resources because the career path went, for example, from system analyst to senior system analyst to team leader. Some of the brightest technical people quit after several years because they did not want to be team leaders, so there were no other promotions coming. While these agencies were successful in attracting talent, they often had trouble retaining it. The intelligence community, on the other hand, was very successful in retaining top quality resources. They were successful for several reasons, not the least of which was the opportunity for employees to work on the absolute, cutting edge of technology. They had developed career paths that enabled technical staff to be promoted all the way to the senior executive level, with comparable pay, without having to be managers. It may be difficult to imagine a resource on a team that you manage making the same or even more money than you, but it is effective and in many ways fair.

If comparable career paths are not available in your company, then you must consider alternatives. When an employee reaches the top of his or her career path, they no longer have incentive to perform and may begin to look for a new job with more opportunity. The ability to transfer to other groups can be effective because it allows employees to expand their skill base, and the other path may have more opportunity for growth.

Training is also a very powerful tool that employees view as opportunity. The ability to expand their professional knowledge is important to many people. Many companies offer tuition or tuition reimbursement to employees. The rules vary by company, but most employees appreciate the opportunity.

12.3.2 Empowerment

Empowerment is a word that has been, unfortunately, used and abused. This is unfortunate because empowering a person or a team is an excellent way to motivate them. In its simplest form, empowerment means giving someone the authority to make decisions without seeking your approval. So what's the big deal? The big deal is that you are providing the person or team the chance to be the masters of their own destiny. When you allow a person or a team to make their own decisions about how they will do their jobs, they may enthusiastically take ownership of their jobs and commit themselves to doing a good job. After all, they want to prove that they deserve that opportunity and that they know what they are doing. They are committed to making their ideas a success. They are committed to working through issues and problems by implementing their own ideas rather than pointing out the problems with someone else's ideas. Empowerment enhances collaboration by giving your teams the authority to get things done in the best way they can. How committed to success are they when they are implementing someone else's ideas?

Empowerment can generate excitement and energy. It is exciting to have the freedom to change your corner of the world and to have the opportunity to make it a success. When a team is empowered, it can be even more exciting because of the synergy empowerment can create amongst the team members. The opportunity to brainstorm ideas and the commitment to make them work can blow new life into a team or a project—or both.

Empowerment also has its weaknesses, so you may have issues to deal with. Not everyone wants to be empowered. Some people do not want to take the risk of failure associated with empowerment. By its very nature, empowerment means giving someone the chance to fail and responsibility for that failure as well. A person or team that is not empowered to make decisions can always say they were just doing what they were told. They can't do that when they are making the decisions. Be aware that not all people want that responsibility and risk. If this is the case, either do not empower that person or do it very slowly and carefully, with generous doses of reassurance.

And what about you? What is your role if people are making their own decisions? Your role hasn't diminished; it has shifted. Instead of making the decisions, you may only review them. Ask questions to make sure the employee or team has considered all aspects of their decisions. Make sure they understand the impact of their decisions on other teams or individuals. Make sure they collaborate with others as necessary. Ensure that company requirements and standards or regulatory requirements are met, and explain the importance of maintaining those standards. This is particularly true when teams don't see or understand the need for certain reporting requirements. Without understanding, they may try to eliminate the filing of certain reports. You need to verify those decisions and explain, if necessary, why it can't be eliminated. Do not discourage them from challenging the need—just be sure they are not violating company policy.

Another significant role for you is to remove roadblocks that may affect your team's progress. You are also the key to communicating changes within your organization and making sure changes flow smoothly.

12.3.3 Challenge

Challenge is an excellent technique for motivating most people. Give people special tasks outside of their normal responsibilities. This helps to break them out of their routines and raises their enthusiasm. Challenge them with a project that goes beyond the scope of their usual responsibilities or with something that has higher visibility than everything else they are doing. You could also give them responsibility for identifying the root cause of a persistent problem. Just be sure to do it carefully, so that you don't put them in a no-win situation. You should always support them through the effort, especially if this is their first "special" project.

Be aware that not all people respond to challenge the same way. Some people are perfectly content with the status quo and may resist new challenges. Others may not respond well to the "pressure" of a new challenge. Some people just can't handle new challenges, so again, think carefully before asking someone to take on a challenge if your main goal is to increase motivation and enthusiasm.

12.3.4 Self-Reviews

Another good technique for keeping your staff motivated is to have them review themselves. Some companies do this only at the specified review time, which can make it difficult to remember all of the good things that employee has done throughout the year. A much more effective technique is to have applicable employees write about the great things they have done in a monthly status report. This keeps your employees focused on the good things they are doing and forces them to think about those things. It also keeps you informed and makes your job easier at review time. Some of the things they can write about include

- Cases where they feel like they "went the extra mile" to help someone

- Times when they came in early or stayed late to figure out a particularly difficult or nagging problem

- Self-training

- Research they performed
- Something new they learned this month

You can even ask them to state the benefit of each of these things to corporation.

This technique keeps your employees focused on going the extra mile and thinking about how they are adding value to the company. It also serves as a reminder to them and to you of all the good things they are doing.

▶ 12.4 The Manager's Role in Motivation

You have the most important role in motivating the staff. You own their motivation, or lack thereof. Your attitude and actions set the tone for the entire staff. You should not think of yourself as a manager; instead, consider yourself a team leader. You set the tone and lead by example on a daily basis. You need to spend time in front of and with your team. It's your job to establish the expectations and demonstrate the enthusiasm needed to meet and exceed them. You must do this every day to establish the culture.

If your organization is going through changes, such as implementing new problem management processes and implementing new tools, your participation is even more important. Your staff needs your support through times of change. They need to understand your vision and see your confidence and enthusiasm This is your opportunity to turn your vision into culture. Yes, there will difficulties and setbacks, but you must lead the team through those. If you don't, who will?

Implementing change is always difficult, but there is much you can do to ensure success. There are several ideas discussed in the following sections that can help you implement changes to your problem management processes. Many of these techniques will be important and should be considered for use even after the changes have been successfully institutionalized.

12.4.1 Expectations

One of the most important things you must do to ensure success is to establish, communicate, and manage expectations of the changes you are implementing. The expectations must be clearly communicated and managed to the hierarchy above you and to your team below you. The best way to communicate expectations is to document and then present them, over and over and over. Focus on communicating all aspects of your vision—not just what will be done, but how you expect it to be done. If you have established measurable goals and objectives, communicate them. Immediately update your documentation any time an expectation changes, and keep the original version. Since you own the project (implementing new problem management processes), you own the expectations, historical and current. It seems that often, no matter how many times you repeat them, many people will not hear them. Something, perhaps their own expectations, will stick in their minds and you will have to cover the expectation history with them.

12.4.2 Training

Train the team in the new processes. Make sure the team understands every step of the new process. Make sure they understand the inputs and outputs of each step. Also, make sure the teams understand the logic behind each step in the process. People have to understand why they are doing something, not just what has to be done. Train them how to work together, the way you see it working, and emphasize cooperation. Use role-playing if necessary, but make sure they see the kind of cooperation you expect and the level that is required to make the new processes work. You most likely do not want business as usual, particularly where collaboration is required. Focus on training your staff on cooperation between teams, what has to be done, and your vision for how it works.

12.4.3 Reassurance and Reinforcement

You're making changes. Changes are always difficult because some people don't like change. Even if no one is opposed to the changes, there is much to be learned and, inevitably, fine-tuning of the processes is required. Training your teams on the new processes is just the first step. You have to reassure your team that you and the rest of management will continue to support them. Mistakes will be made during the transition. You must expect it and let your team know that you expect it and that it is okay. Make sure your teams know that you will all learn from the mistakes and that you are willing to make changes as necessary, based on what you have learned from the mistakes. The team's ideas are critical to success, so listen to them as they go through this process. Also, make sure the people you report to understand that there will be problems and ensure that they will continue to support the effort.

Any time that you implement something new, make sure experts are available on the spot at all times to reinforce what should be done and how it should be done. Remember, during and immediately after the transition is your best opportunity to establish a new culture. Be there for your staff when they have questions or need clarification. Don't just tell them what to do; tell them why it is important. This will reinforce the vision and help them to learn, not just to memorize.

12.4.4 Enthusiasm

Implementing change can be very frustrating for all involved. To make your new processes work, your teams must not only understand the new processes, they must be enthusiastic about making them work. There are a number of different ways to do this. You must maintain your enthusiasm throughout, even during times of frustration and doubt. Lead by example.

Another good approach with teams is to develop some good, healthy competition between teams. Competition between teams will cause members of each team to bond and will build enthusiasm. Give your teams names, even if it's as simple as Red and Green. To make this work, you must reward the teams either with recognition or cash, or both. Generally, teams respond best to recognition. Recognize your teams with trophies, plaques, or in the company newsletter.

You must base the competition on metrics. If you don't, and if you use purely subjective measure, your competition and the enthusiasm will be an instant failure. Think about it. If you are competing and rules and criteria for winning are not specified, how do you know your ranking? How do you know that the winner really did do a better job than you? How do you know where to focus your efforts? The bottom line is that if you can't specify the criteria and how to measure success, you, as the manager, haven't determined what is important for your teams to focus on and probably haven't done a good job of setting expectations. If you can't determine what is important for your teams to focus on, how can you expect them to know where to focus? Unless you're very lucky, there is no way your teams can be successful. You have to tell them what is important and how you will measure their success in order for them to accomplish their goals. In and of itself, this often builds a better, more enthusiastic work environment because people want to know how they will be measured.

Because you are keeping metrics, post interim results in a public place so that each team knows where they stand compared to their peers. When you have picked your winner, let that team take a leadership role in telling other teams how they became the best. They are proud of their accomplishments, and they must share their techniques with the other teams. Sharing with other teams is the healthy part of the competition.

Here's an example of what happens when you don't use metrics. A vice president at ABCD company decided to implement an employee of the month program. He did this for all the right reasons—to recognize the hard work and extraordinary efforts of certain members of his staff. Further, he wanted to encourage other members of his staff to follow that example. However, the program was a total failure. There are several reasons the program failed. First, the group he was rewarding was a highly educated group of consultants that spent a lot of time on their own in front of clients. Employee of the month seemed a bit juvenile because we are used to seeing this at fast food restaurants and hotels everywhere. Second, there was no criteria, or at least no hard criteria, such as metrics, to use as guideposts. The criteria seemed to be happy client versus unhappy client and Mr. VP's perception of how hard the individual worked. We all know that some clients are always unhappy, no matter what, so this soft measure was not necessarily a reflection of what the employee of the month accomplished. Second, visibility is the worst way to measure performance because it forces some team members to do whatever it takes to be visible. Often, this means that visibility is the only thing they focus on, while others are doing the work. Worse, when Mr. VP was "fooled" by that visibility, his team instantly lost respect for him. It showed that he was completely out of touch with what was really happening in his department. He was labeled "clueless." The program was a complete joke around the company and dismissed as being anything to strive for. It was too frequent, it was the wrong type of program for the professionals involved, and there was no measurable criteria. The point is that if you plan to implement competition, make sure you use rock-solid metrics, or your program will likely fail, or worse, it could be a disincentive and cause your staff to lose respect for you.

12.4.5 Measurement

As mentioned above, metrics are the key to success. As the manager, you own the success or failure of the organization, so it is up to you to define success. Establish measurable goals and objectives for the organization. Break high-level organizational goals and objectives into smaller team-level goals and objectives. Your organization achieves its goals based on the contribution of your teams, so define what teams have to accomplish. If you can't measure it, don't bother setting it as a goal or objective.

As the manager, you are now faced with some difficult decisions on setting targets. You are implementing new processes, so you may not have historical data to base your targets on. So what do you do? At this point, you should have defined what it means to be successful. Many companies do this based on what their peers are doing. For example, suppose your peer service centers resolve 85 percent of their calls during the initial contact. Set that as a target. You still do not have historical data to base your targets on, but at least you have a goal to begin measuring against. Start measuring immediately, and after one or two quarters, review your goals and make realistic adjustments to the targets. You can still use first-level resolution as a metric to foster competition between first-level teams. Gather the data and publish it. You may need to adjust your processes if you find that, after measuring for the first two quarters, you are far from the goal. You could empower your competing teams to find a better way. Meet with and share this information with your team, both in the beginning and during the reviews. Make sure the team knows that the first set of targets are merely a SWAG (sophisticated wild-ass guess) and that once metrics are gathered, better targets will be established. This is critical in the beginning.

When teams know what is expected of them and they can measure what they have achieved, they are self-motivated and self-directed.

12.4.6 Daily Meetings

When implementing new processes, you should consider holding daily meetings with your team or with your team leaders. The primary purpose is to provide leadership to your team during this critical time. As mentioned earlier, reassuring your team through periods of change is critical to their success.

The purpose of the daily meeting can vary, depending on what is happening within your organization. For the purposes of this book, let's assume you are implementing new problem management processes. When you are implementing your new processes, questions about those processes will come up every day, particularly right after you cut over from the old to the new. No matter how well documented and prepared you are in advance of implementing the new processes, issues will arise. The daily meeting is your chance to meet with your key leaders to address those issues and answer those questions. If you don't know the answer, say so, and brainstorm with the group. Leave the meeting with a new answer that everyone present heard.

If your teams interface during the course of their work, that is, if the outputs of one team is the input to one or more other teams, this will be a possible source of questions right after cut-over to the new processes. Typically, interface issues include such items as what format the output will be in, where it will be stored, when it will be available, and who has access to it. These are all basically critical workflow and collaboration issues. Once the workflow and collaboration issues have been worked out and have been in practice, the content of the output will most likely evolve. Assuming team 2 receives the output from team 1, team 2 may find that modifications to the output from team 1 would greatly enhance their ability to perform their work. During the daily meeting, the team 2 leader should raise the issue and the benefits of the proposed changes. The team 1 leader should address any problems with making the changes and either agree to the changes, agree to evaluate the changes, or disagree. As the manager, you may have to make the final decision. The key is to make the decision, convey the logic behind your decision, document it, and move on.

The daily meeting is also a great time to bring up innovations. If one team has made a change to their process that improves performance, the team leader should share that with the other team leaders. This allows the other team leaders to make adjustments as well and to discuss any concerns they may have.

Your team leaders are responsible for communicating changes back to their team and making sure their team implements the agreed upon changes. If problems arise in implementing the changes, they must be discussed during the next daily meeting.

The daily meeting should also address process issues wholly owned by one team. You might think that since it doesn't affect the other teams, why not deal with it independently, in some forum other than the daily meeting. There are several benefits to addressing the issue during the daily meeting. First and foremost, you and your team leaders are a team. Opening up and sharing issues helps to build esprit de corps. It allows your teams to brainstorm and help each other. It affords your team leaders a chance to build trust and depend on each other. It gives your team leaders peers to work with. It allows your team leaders to understand each other's processes and workflow.

In some cases, you may agree that the issue is best addressed outside of the daily meeting. If this is the case, and the issue was brought up during the daily meeting, the eventual outcome should be shared with the rest of team leaders.

12.4.7 Your Role in the Daily Meeting

Your role as the leader of the organization is to lead the daily meeting. There are a number of key factors to making the daily meeting successful. If possible, hold the meeting at the same time in the same conference room every day. This stresses the importance you place on the meeting. It ensures your team leaders that they have the opportunity and a forum to meet with their peers and you each day. The meeting provides the right time and place to deal with issues. Do not underestimate the value of being consistent.

Consider setting the meeting for late afternoon. This allows you to address all the issues on the day they arise, while they are still fresh. Your team leaders will get in the habit of keeping an issue list for the daily meeting. They know their issues will be addressed and resolved, and they communicate that assurance back to their teams. Very few issues, if any, fall through the cracks. The daily meeting allows your team leaders to be successful leaders. Their team members know that any issues they raise will be addressed by their team leader in the daily meeting. Your team leaders can also tell the team the logic behind the decision, not just the decision. Team members need to understand decisions if they are to maintain respect for their management. The entire organization develops confidence in the management structure.

Most people attend so many fruitless meetings during the day that the thought of a new daily meeting will not be well received. It is your job as the owner of this meeting to change all that. You accomplish that by being a leader, not a manager. Set the tone of the meetings during the first meeting and consistently reinforce it every day. The overall tone should be that the meetings are short, concise, extremely focused, important, and valuable. As the leader, you need to project that tone in everything you say and do during the meeting. You have to believe it for your team to believe it.

Keep the meeting short. You and your team leaders have other work to do. The only way a daily meeting can be successful is if it is short. Try to limit the meeting to 30 minutes. This may be very difficult at first, because your team may never have attended meetings that were so focused they could accomplish something in 30 minutes. Discuss the 30-minute rule with your team during the first meeting and make sure everyone understands and agrees to it. One key to keeping the meetings to 30 minutes is not to develop a backlog of issues. This is possible, because you have the meetings every day and you must resolve issues every day during the meeting. This sets the tone of the meetings.

The entire focus of the meeting is on process. Give each team leader a chance to address what is and what is not working. Each team's status and progress toward goals, at the highest level, may be addressed during the meeting only if it brings up process-related issues. There is not time during the daily meeting to have detailed status reviews. Further, status reviews are not the point of the meeting. Establish during the first meeting that the daily meetings are not a forum for bitching and moaning. There is no time for that in a 30-minute meeting. As the facilitator, it is your job to keep the meeting focused on process. If the conversation begins to move away from process, politely but firmly stop it and bring it back into focus. You are the only one who can keep the meeting to 30 minutes, and your team will rely on you to do that.

Don't let them down. After awhile, your team will develop these positive meeting habits, and you will not have to intervene as much.

These meetings are short, so they must start on time. Lead by example and never, ever be late for a meeting. Let other team members know that being late is unacceptable behavior. Start the meetings on time, even if someone is late, and discuss that tardiness in private, after the meeting. If you don't start the meeting on time, you are making other team members wait, and you will either exceed or cut into the 30-minute limit. If you cannot be there, appoint someone to facilitate the meeting in your stead.

In setting the tone, make sure that the meetings are nonthreatening. You must know all of the issues in order to resolve them. If the team feels that raising an issue will result in criticism or negative opinion of their performance, they will be reluctant to raise the issue. Set the tone such that team leaders know this is where they go for help. Make sure that your team understands that you expect issues and that the purpose of the daily meeting is to raise and resolve them. When issues are presented, ask the rest of the team to brainstorm solutions. Ask everyone for their opinions and give everyone the chance to express ideas. Do not tolerate personal attacks or lack of mutual respect. If that occurs during the meeting, stop it in mid-sentence and reinforce that it is not allowed.

Finally, do not allow sidebar conversations. Allow only one person to speak at a time. This is just common courtesy and is essential for mutual respect. If a sidebar occurs, it is your job as facilitator to stop it. Keep a list of issues to be resolved. If during a meeting an issue is raised and the interested parties decide to resolve it outside of the daily meeting, ask for the results the next day. Do not let issues slide. If necessary, force the team leaders to take the time to resolve the issue. This is especially important when the issue deals with processes, because it is better to deal with changes to the new processes as soon as possible, before the rest of the team becomes too indoctrinated with the current process. Also, you do not want to create a backlog of issues. Keep a record of the decisions made during meetings. If four or five decisions are made every day, it is very difficult after a week to remember them all. Most of the decisions made during the meeting will be process related and should be implemented immediately. Because the decisions should be put into practice immediately, it will not be as important to have them documented for the sake of remembering them. It may be more important to recall the logic behind the decision.

The daily meetings have many benefits, as we've discussed. There are other benefits as well. Your team leaders will be busy all day, managing their teams. You and your team leaders are a team, and the daily meetings give you the opportunity to work and feel like a team. If you don't have the daily meeting, how often are all the members together? It is hard to feel like a team if you only get together once a week. You have probably also encouraged some competition between teams. Having the daily meetings will keep that competition under control and remind your team leaders that they too are part of a team.

The daily meetings also allow for better understanding throughout your organization. Your team leaders will know from the daily meetings what each of the other teams are doing, the processes they use, the issues they face, and more importantly, why they are conducting business in a certain way. This is important because when one of their team members has an issue with another team, the team leader can explain the other team's position. Each team leader can communicate back to their team any changes that need to be made, what other teams are doing, and most importantly, why the other teams are doing what they are doing. This results in a coordinated effort to achieve the organization's goals.

Meetings can somehow take on a life of their own, and they often tend to get out of control. They get onto a path and it can be difficult to bring them back into focus. As the leader and facilitator of the meeting, you are generally responsible for keeping the meeting focused and under control. Even you will have days when you don't do a very good job of this, and even you may get off track in the meeting. Therefore, it is important to allow your team to have some control of the meeting. Remember, you are a member of the team too, not a dictator, and just like the rest of the team, you'll have good and bad days. There are many different techniques available; some work and some do not. One technique that works quite well is to document the meeting rules and distribute copies, or even better, post them prominently in the conference room where everyone can read them. Allow, even encourage, any member of the team to point out a rule if they feel it is being broken.

When meetings get out of focus, it is often very difficult to bring them back on track. This is especially true if you're the one taking it down the wrong path. One effective way to stop the procession down the wrong path is by using a visual aid. While it may at first seem silly, a visual aid manages to catch everyone's attention, thus stopping the meeting and subsequently allowing the meeting to get back on track. An example of an effective visual aid is a bottle of Scope®. Everyone on the team chuckles at how silly an idea it is when you first put the bottle on the table. When the chuckling is finished, tell everyone that they have the right to knock the bottle over (get a plastic bottle) if they feel that the meeting is off track. When the bottle is knocked over, stop immediately and let the person that knocked it over explain his or her view on why the meeting is off track. Make a decision as a group on how to proceed. Try it and you will be surprised at how effective it is. It is really effective when one or two people tend to dominate the discussion, because it is a polite and nonthreatening way for other, less-aggressive individuals to get the meeting back in focus. The key is that when the bottle is knocked over, the meeting must stop until the issue is addressed.

Another effective visual aid is a small yellow piece of fabric, like that used by a referee in a football game. Again, it may seem silly, but it is effective. Everyone attending the meeting gets a flag. Like whiteboard markers and other conference room tools that are used on a regular basis, the flags should be left in the meeting room. When a team member feels that a rule has been broken or that the meeting is getting out of scope, he or she simply tosses the flag onto the table and the meeting stops immediately until the issue is addressed. Unlike sporting events, no penalties are ever assessed. The point is not to penalize but to stick to the rules. In one company, the person with the most flags by Thursday had to bring bagels or doughnuts on Friday for the office. This was acceptable, and worked only because flags were not related to performance and no one perceived the flags as a personal attack. The members were very good-natured and functioned very well as a team.

Use these approaches during and after implementation of new processes. You will greatly increase your chances of successfully implementing the processes and creating a new culture.

Index

process 88, 92, 94–96, 101, 103
reactive 5, 6, 36, 37, 41
work restoration 90

Q

queuing theory 13–15, 106

R

referral
    agreement 49
    follow-up 53
    metrics 69
    value-added 2, 46–49, 53, 69
remote control
    applying resolutions 98
    benefits 87, 162, 189, 194
    data gathering 93
    implementation 195
    permission 87, 93, 98
    resistance 184, 194
    tools 194, 203, 207
    use 87, 88, 207
    versus dispatch 162
resource loading. *See also* queuing
    theory
    multiple pools 15–17
    multiple tiers 18
    optimizing 6, 13–15, 20–22
    workforce management 185, 189,
    194

S

security
    customer validation 9, 46, 48, 50
    escalation 92
    organizing for 21, 22
    prioritizing requests 81

service
    catalog 4, 5, 110, 178
    contracts. *See* service level agree-
        ment
    on-demand 1, 5
    scope of 4, 67, 204, 217
    value added 2, 4, 8, 16, 69
service center
    charter 1, 2, 4, 58
    external 3
    internal 3
    objectives 13, 66, 137–143, 150,
        172, 183, 210, 219, 222
    type 13, 138, 163
service center objectives
    baseline data 141, 142
    creating 137–140, 142, 143
    customer satisfaction 144
    employee 222
    expectations 219
    for selecting tools 183
    managing 140
    measuring 141, 222
    metrics 140, 141, 144, 150
    motivation 210
service delivery
    immediate 13–15, 22, 38, 186,
        187, 201
    managed 6, 13, 22
    mode 5
    problem determination 86, 91
    type 5, 6, 13
    work restoration 85, 90, 91
service levels
    defining 4, 5, 25, 26, 108, 112
    improving 140, 173
    organizing to meet 13
service level agreements
    content 177
    defining 26, 175, 177

T

W

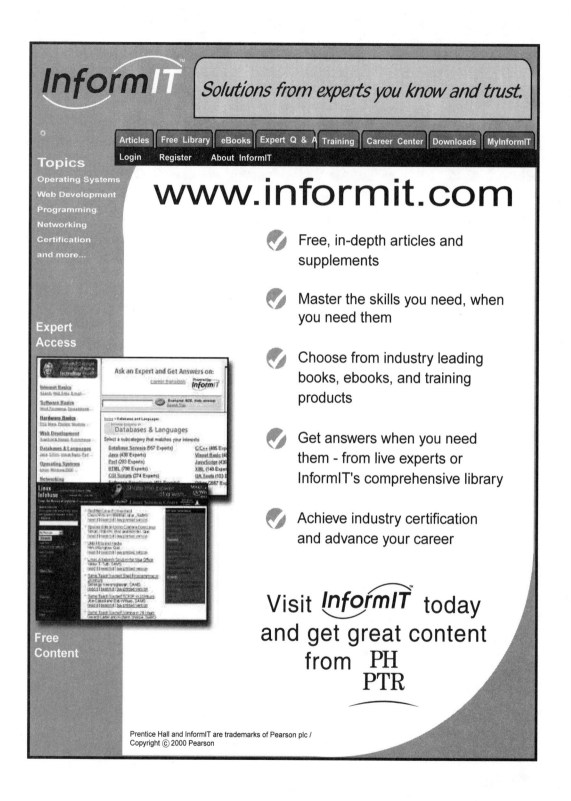